Barney Lacendre was the best trapper in the woods. He could put meat on his table every day. When Barney set his traps, he nearly always got results.

Yet for a month funny things had been happening on Barney's trapline. Like every trap being sprung and not a track in the snow around them. And always they were empty.

Barney was sure he was the victim of a trapline curse. The power of evil spirits was focused on him. But what was he to do?

THE BUSHMAN

AND

THE SPIRITS

THE BUSHMAN

AND

THE SPIRITS

by
Barney Lacendre

as told to
Owen Salway

HORIZON HOUSE PUBLISHERS
Beaverlodge, Alberta, Canada

ISBN 0-88965-033-0

HORIZON BOOKS
are published by Horizon House Publishers
Box 600, Beaverlodge, Alberta TOH OCO
Printed in Canada

DEDICATED

TO

THE GLORY OF GOD

About the Author

Owen Salway was born in Spy Hill, Saskatchewan. A graduate of the Briercrest Bible Institute, Caronport, Saskatchewan, he joined the Northern Canada Evangelical Mission, of which he has been a member for the past twenty-nine years. At present he serves as an Editor of **Northern Lights**, the official publication of NCEM.

Owen is the author of some 200 published works, both as a free-lance writer and on assignments. His works include two books, **Reach for Tomorrow** and **The Tender Years**, compilations of Christian stories for teens.

His articles and stories have appeared in such publications as **The Good News Broadcaster, The Gospel Herald & Sunday School Times, Teen Power,** and **Sunday-Pix.** In addition, he has written for Standard Publishing, Harvest Publishing, Concordia Publishing, Mennonite Publishing and other firms.

Barney Lacendre, subject of **The Bushman And The Spirits,** is a choice and personal friend of Mr. Salway.

Mr. Salway is the victim of Muscular Dystrophy.

Author's Note

The facts in this book are as accurate as the memory of those involved can make them. There is no fiction except for certain connective materials, dialogues that had to be reconstructed and the changing of the names of certain individuals. They were changed rather than risk offending unintentionally. But the people are real. If there are errors in the book, they are not included by design.

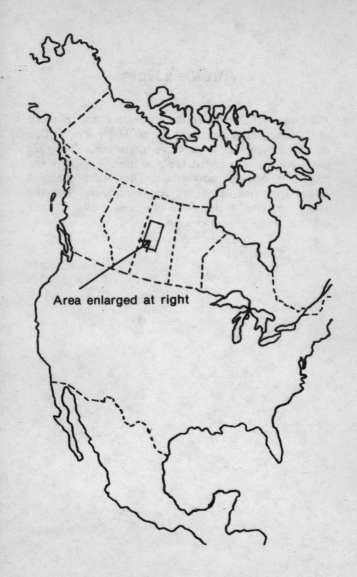

Area enlarged at right

Barney's Location in Canada

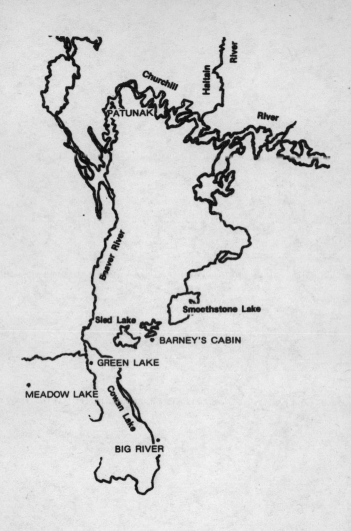

Map of Barney's Travels

Contents

Foreword

I first met Barney Lacendre years ago; shortly after he became a Christian. He was a great, towering man with a crew cut, a winning smile and the calm assurance that God would sustain him in any difficulty.

"When Barney came to Christ," missionary Marshall Calverley said of him, "he put aside the things of the world and has never looked back." That is as true today as it was six months after his conversion.

Barney is known and respected by both the white and Indian population all through northern Saskatchewan. His hunting skills and great strength are legendary among those who have known him best. He is a wise man, for all of his lack of formal education, and has won many of his people to the Lord—some who were in their eighties.

I know of no one more worthy of having a book written about him, or anyone more suitable to write it than Owen Salway. Owen has known Barney from the beginning of his Christian experience, has been his neighbor, has counselled him and joked and fellowshipped with him for endless hours over many years, as good friends do.

I am sure you will find Barney as warm and exciting and devoted to the Lord Jesus Christ as my wife and I have. He is a great Christian friend and brother. It is a privilege to get to know him.

Bernard Palmer

Introduction

In the mid-sixties a young Indian man in a northern village was suddenly stricken with severely crossed eyes. Both eyes were turned in to such a degree that the pupils were barely visible. He needed help to walk about. He was sent outside to a hospital in Saskatoon, Saskatchewan, where for two months he puzzled twenty-two doctors by his unusual condition. Shortly after he returned to the village, his condition unchanged, he sat in our home and bitterly remarked, "I know who did this to me, and we're going to fix him."

The next time I saw him his eyes were perfectly normal and they are still straight today. Although I didn't get the story from him, another person in the village informed me that the young man and his stepfather had taken their guns to a certain cabin and threatened to shoot the occupant unless the hex was removed. Another man of this same village told me about getting up morning after morning with both his legs and hips beaten black and blue by spirit forces set in motion by a hex that had been put on him by a man sixty miles away in another village.

In the Book of Revelation, chapter 2 and verse 24, John speaks about the things of Satan and says two things about them. One, there are things of Satan that are **deep**; that is, they are covered, hidden, and not known by normal perception. The other thing he says is that these deep things of Satan have to be **learned**. Whether by the Indians back in the bush, the priests of the Voodoo or Vodun religion in Haiti, the Red monks of Tibet or the modern occultist on the college campus, there must be a time of concentrated learning. There are sessions of specific teaching by those who possess the secrets. There are rigid rules governing formulae and recipes, all intricately laid out and followed as humans intrude into deep Satanic things clearly forbidden by God in His Word.

The North American Indians have learned to use the power of evil spirits to a very great and frightening degree. Because these things are dark, hidden, and very illegal, they are seldom spoken of, especially to outsiders. In most cases they are stoutly denied. So, when one who has been wonderfully delivered from the dominion of darkness and translated into the Kingdom of God's beloved Son comes forward, and shares the deep secrets of dark practices, we should take heed and pay attention.

After having spent twenty-seven years as a missionary among northern Indian tribes, I am aware that behind the unaccountable fear, the deep bondage, the inability to accept Jesus Christ, lies a dark curse brought about by years of learning the deep things of Satan. I have been attacked by these malevolent spirits. Wild and frightening dreams have disturbed my sleep. I have heard supernatural noises, been palpably grasped in an encounter, had my mind assaulted and endured diabolical temptation.

Other missionaries have reported similar things. Some have smelled odors, others have heard noises of activity when no human was around. Still others have experienced palls of deep darkness moving toward them in the night. All who would bring Christ's redeeming message of release to these souls encounter these things in varying degrees and kinds. These oppositions all speak the same thing to us: i.e., evil beings of the unseen world are here who hate Christ and His gospel and they have gained a deep foothold in many lives.

You may prefer to disbelieve much of what is written in the following account. Your rejection may be based on the incredulous nature of many of the stories here related. It must be borne in mind, though, that Satan works in lying signs and wonders. It is often very difficult for one to tell where the real leaves off and the visionary begins. However, for the purposes of those involved that is hardly the point. The power touched is real power, however illegal it may be. And the ends of those visionary or real encounters are very tangible. For example, the one who uses a love potion actually ends up with a flesh and blood person desperate to be with him. He who engages in placing a murder hex actually ends up with his enemy dead. Real animals are killed by these practices and are eaten. Bodies are actually teleported miles through the air and have either to walk back or use some other mode of transportion.

In the Yukon a man who is now a fine Christian told me that before he came to Christ, he knew several men who gave their souls to the devil so they could learn to play the violin or guitar. He said they could then play immediately and very skillfully, but added that they were bad men. He then told me a very beautiful sequel. One day he remarked to his wife that they needed some music in their services and that he thought Jesus could do greater things than the devil. He then proceeded to purchase an accordion, sat down, closed his eyes and prayed, "Lord Jesus, You are greater than the devil. We need music for our meetings. We used to give ourselves to the devil before. Now I give all of myself to You. Let me play this accordion." I, and others, have on several occasions attended those meetings and heard him play. He sits with eyes closed, and plays any gospel chorus or hymn being sung.

I commend this book to you. It is very timely. It comes just when hundreds of native people are turning to Jesus Christ and many others are seriously considering doing so. It also appears at a time when Indian religion is becoming more open, prominent and powerful. Reports coming to me from the fields tell of missionaries uncovering an ever-increasing amount of startling and fearful evidence of long-standing spirit bondage. May the Holy Spirit use this book to open your eyes to the real cause of the Indians' condition and lostness. May it drive you to prayer to help in their release as you understand that cruel Pharaohs and numberless unseen taskmasters hold evil sway over the tribes of North America's native people. Let it show you how God can and does, through Jesus Christ, effect His great deliverance from all bondage, spirits and sin.

L.W. Elford, Western Field Director,
Northern Canada Evangelical Mission

1

The Trapline Hex

When you're a drunkard and your credit is no good and your grub box is about empty, you start wondering what's gone wrong.

I'd done plenty of wondering the day I tramped back to my cabin shouldering the last string of traps from my trapline. The snow-laden spruce trees edging the trail like a jewelled necklace held no beauty for me that day. Neither did the velvet-tufted bulrushes poking their heads through the snow catch my attention. My heart was heavy. I'd done a lot of guessing and hoping, but the purpose had gone from my footsteps and my stride was slow.

I was a trapper; maybe not the best in the world, but I was the best in this part of Saskatchewan. Nobody argued with me over that. I was good enough to have meat on my table every day.

I'm a bushman; born and raised in the bush. I've had American big game hunters flock in like birds in the fall, almost standing in line, waiting for me to guide them. So I knew something was the matter when I set traps for a month with no luck. Funny things were happening on my trapline; like every trap being sprung and not a single track around them on the snow.

My trapline was isolated—so people weren't springing my traps. It was the spirits. I know the powers of witchcraft. In fact, I was a witch doctor myself, trained by some of the best witch doctors in the north. I'll tell you things about witchcraft that you'll find hard to believe. Things I've seen with my own eyes.

So that day, heading back to my cabin, under leaden skies, I knew the power of the spirits was centered on me. It was like walking under a threatening thundercloud.

I was under a witchcraft hex. A curse that had already emptied my grub box and left my wallet as thin as a piece of birchbark.

Witchcraft isn't something that's just practiced in distant heathen countries. It's going on right now, here in Canada. It's widespread, maybe more so now than ever before. It isn't just back in the bush, either. It comes in different forms. Look, right here in this town, thousands of people go to bingo games. They come from all over. But where are the major prizes, like trucks, boats and trailers going? Beginning a year or two ago, they started going to a settlement north of here. I believe with all my heart that witchcraft may be involved. From my experience with witchcraft, it is a small matter for the spirits to have the right numbers tumble from the machine.

I'm not a man who gets all churned up inside when trouble crowds me off the bush trail. I grew up tough and I've stepped on the heads of a lot of troubles as though they were insects. But I've got feelings like everybody else and those feelings were running

24

pretty deep by the time I reached my shack nestled under the tall spruce.

Shoving the crude door of my log cabin open, I lumbered inside. My 280-pound frame draped in heavy parka and sweater left little room for my huge, stuffed chair I had brought from the south as a touch of luxury, my single cot and my wooden table.

Jerking the traps off my shoulders, I threw them on the pile at the foot of my bed. Resentment surfaced in me as I stood looking down at them. Along with my rifle, those traps represented my means of making a living. Every trap from my 24-square-mile trapline lay at my feet. The curse covered my trapline like the snow covered the ground.

Pushing the parka hood back off my head, I turned my attention to the heavy, squat cookstove that looked even to me as though it had occupied that spot from eternity past. My cabin had been vacant since morning and was little warmer on the inside than the frigid temperature beyond the log walls.

Within fifteen minutes the stove had crackled its way through enough split spruce to enable me to shed my parka and start thinking about my stomach. It had been a good month since the curse had been put on my trapline. A month without furs, meat or income. I pulled my grub box out from under the table. It was low, but I'd gone without food when necessary before. About every kind of animal in the north has laid on my plate, including skunk and squirrel, so I wasn't stuck yet. During the depression in the 30s I had to trap squirrels and sell their hides for seven cents each in order to make ends meet.

Still, this was January and I didn't know yet whether the hex extended beyond my trapline or not. Perhaps my rifle would be as useless as my traps. If so, there would be no meat or fur. I'd know the answer to that soon.

Though I had never stooped to begging, I suppose that possibility was open, though unlikely, as few people ever ventured into my area on the shores of Smoothstone Lake in northern Saskatchewan.

It was with some curiosity, then, that I heard a vehicle approaching. Rubbing the frost from my window I saw a truck jerk to a stop a short distance from my cabin. I recognized the lanky, long-striding individual as he came along the trail. It was the missionary, Marshall Calverley, from Dore Lake. I knew him a little. He stopped by once in a while on his mail-haul between Dore and Big River.

I shoved the door open, letting in a cloud of frigid air that swept across the floor in billows. The missionary ducked his head under the doorframe and stepped in.

"How are you making out, Barney?"

He removed his mitt and shook my hand.

"No good." My reply was abrupt.

"What do you mean?"

"There's a curse on my trapline. I'm going to go hungry," I told him, extending my lower lip toward the pile of traps at the foot of my cot.

The missionary watched me without speaking for the space of a few moments. He was smart in the ways of Indians. I remembered now that he had once told me he was a fur buyer for the Hudson's Bay Company in northern Ontario. Maybe he knew something of hexes.

"It started about a month ago," I said, feeding the stove a few more pieces of split spruce. "I saw some treaty Indians from the south go by my cabin about that time. I guess they saw my furs hanging outside and heard what a good trapper I was. You see, I'm not a treaty Indian but I'm known throughout the north as a good hunter. Indians get awful jealous when it comes to trapping and hunting. I guess they got a witch doctor to put a curse on my traps." I took off my siwash sweater as the heat built up in the small cabin and eased myself into my overstuffed chair.

Patches of red glowed on top of the stove, more noticeable in the gathering darkness. Getting up, I filled the kerosene lamp and touched a match to the wick. With the kettle now steaming I offered the missionary a cup of tea.

We sat drinking in silence.

"It must have been a powerful witch doctor to put a curse on my traps," I said finally, renewing the conversation.

Flickering orange shadows danced on the walls of the dingy cabin.

"I know what you mean," put in Marshall at last. "I've seen trapline hexes before. I've seen people go hungry. I believe every word you've told me."

I felt good to hear Marshall say that. My heart felt a little bit lighter. It's not very often an Indian can share things like this with a white man. I'll say this for the missionary. He treated me good.

"I'm a witch doctor myself," I ventured, watching for some indication of disapproval. There was none. Still, why should there be? The Indian needs a religion as well as the white man. It's only right and fair.

There was a plan needling the back of my mind for the last few days and it struck me that this would be as good a time as any to put it into action. I turned my attention back to the missionary.

"Any chance of hooking a ride with you next time you go to Big River?" I knew this mail-run took him past there every week.

He nodded. Still, there was nothing unusual about my request. He'd taken me along to Big River before when I wanted to replenish my grubstake. He was with the Northern Canada Evangelical Mission and the mail-run was sort of a sideline.

"I'll be going on Tuesday, Barney, same as usual. I'll stop by your cabin about eight in the morning."

There was no need for the missionary to turn off the main road. I was at the fork-off trail waiting for him at eight sharp. I was always on time. I'd rather walk than wait.

As the truck ground to a halt on the snow-packed road, I tossed a few traps into the cab and heaved myself in after them. I took a crumpled brown paper bag from my pocket, laid it by my feet and settled back. As the isolated snow-covered landscape unravelled beneath the grip tires I could feel the missionary's eyes wandering occasionally to my traps. I thought I'd better offer him the courtesy of an explanation since I was taking a lift from him.

"I'm heading for Whitefish reserve about thirty-five miles south of Big River," I put in as starters.

Marshall nodded and turned his attention back to the road.

"I have a friend there who is a powerful witch doctor. I'll get him to mix up some dope and put it on my traps to break the curse."

The missionary made no reply, but I could tell he was turning it over in his mind. I thought it would be good to strengthen my case. Shifting my lunch bag away from my feet, I turned to face Marshall.

"That witch doctor is so powerful," I said, "that if you lose anything, he will find it."

The missionary's eyebrows raised slightly.

"You make him a little teepee," I continued, "fix a fire inside, put rocks in the fire and pour water on the rocks when they get hot. The witch doctor goes in there and sits in the steam for a while. When he comes out he will tell you where the thing is you lost. It could be anything; a horse, wallet, gun, anything."

I felt relieved when Marshall offered no resistance to my plans. He was a good man after all. The warmth of the cab and the rhythmic sound of the engine made my eyelids heavy and my head nodded occasionally.

"Barney."

My head jerked toward the missionary.

"If I were you, Barney, I wouldn't go to see that witch doctor."

I knew there was more coming once he got started.

"Look, you're going down to the treaty Indians and they'll laugh at you. They'll say, 'You're a non-treaty and can't even look after yourself. You have to come to us for help.' You know how it is between treaty and non-treaty, Barney. Maybe this is the same witch doctor who put the curse on you to start with."

I hadn't really thought about it like that. Marshall knew the Indian way of life pretty good. But maybe this time it was better to be laughed at than go hungry. When you're under a curse you'll do anything to get free. Only an Indian would know what I mean.

"Barney, wait until Sunday, if you don't mind. My son and I will come over to your cabin and pray over your traps. My Father in heaven is well able to grant us a blessing. I'm His child. I belong to the family of God. He will listen to me. When Jesus was on earth He cast out demons, so He knows all about such things."

Well, I didn't think much of that speech. I hadn't met anybody who was more powerful than the witch doctors. I had used the beads and prayed to the white man's God lots of times, but He'd never done anything for me. I'd heard too many stories from the white man, and the Indian didn't usually turn out to be the winner.

We travelled on, neither speaking.

I knew Marshall wasn't finished yet. He was kind of a persistent guy. He turned to me as soon as the truck stopped at Big River.

"How much money have you got, Barney?"

"Six dollars." I didn't tell him that I needed that to buy the witch doctor some tobacco and a nice piece of print cloth for mixing up the dope and getting me out from under the curse.

Marshall opened his wallet and passed me a twenty-dollar bill. That was a lot in those days.

"Here, Barney, buy yourself some groceries." He looked me right in the eyes. "Now, look, I'll be heading back to Dore in a couple of hours. You think over what I said and come back with me if you want." He turned and left.

I fingered the money. "I'll pay you back," I called after him. I did too. I never like to owe anybody anything.

I hit across the street to the cafe and bought myself a good square meal. With the money left I got myself a nice grubstake. All the time I was thinking, "What will I do? Would I take a chance on Marshall's God, which seemed pretty hopeless, or should I use my thumb and catch a ride south to see the witch doctor?"

Well, since I had about a week's supply of food to take back to my cabin, I thought I'd do what the missionary said. If his plan didn't work I could always come back the next week to see the witch doctor. This way it would keep the missionary happy and assure me of any future rides I might need from him.

I was standing by Marshall's truck when he came out of the post office. He didn't let on he was happy, but I could read his face pretty good. It was dark by the time he dropped me off at the forks leading to my cabin and went on to Dore some twenty miles down the road.

Sure enough, come Sunday there was the sound of the truck. I didn't bother looking out the window. It would be Marshall. If he said something he always did it. I pushed the door open when the sound of the footsteps told me they were at the cabin.

Marshall's son, Ron, entered first, followed by the missionary.

"How are you making out, Barney?" Marshall's eyes darted around the cabin, coming to rest on the pile of traps by my cot.

I said, "My stomach is full anyway."

"Got all your traps here, Barney?"

I stirred them around a little with the toe of my moccasin. Some of the springs were broken. "Yeah, this is the lot," I told him. "See this spring? It's broken. That's what happens sometimes when a curse is put on traps. Sometimes the traps have sticks in them, too. I don't know why it is."

We talked for a while and then Marshall knelt down

on the floor. He said, "Barney, you kneel there and Ron can kneel over there."

He started to pray just like I'm talking to you. I never heard a man pray like that before. It wasn't a prayer that you say over and over again. It was his own words. Sometimes he mentioned traps, sometimes Jesus, or Indians. He prayed for quite a while. It was a powerful prayer.

Finally he got up and stepped to the pile of traps. Picking one up, he held it in his hand. He didn't pray out loud but I could tell he was praying, all right. I didn't know what I should do so I just stood waiting. After a time he dropped the trap back on the pile and turned toward me.

"Barney, tomorrow go out and set your traps again."

2

The Test

Frost crystals hung in the air cutting visibility down to a dozen yards as I crowded my way through the cabin door and out into the sub-zero temperature. The crisp air felt good!

There was a flicker of hope in my heart as I thought back to the missionary's prayer. He'd given me a Cree Bible, too, and I'd slept with it under my pillow. Some kind of power crowded in on me a bit when I listened to Marshall's strong words. It was a feeling that hadn't touched me before. At any rate, I would soon know whether there was anything to it.

I glanced around at the freshly fallen snow to see if any animals had ventured near my cabin during the night. I saw none.

Northern winters heightened my love for the country. A good many times out on the trail I've hobbled my horse, laid down a few feed bales and slept under the stars when it was thirty degrees below zero. Sometimes when I'd poke my head out of the sleeping bag in the morning, I'd be under a blanket of snow. I liked that!

Grabbing my snowshoes from against the cabin, I

strapped them on. The frosty crunch of snow beneath them was my only thermometer. It told me I was in for a cold day on the trapline. Snowshoes were essential in keeping my 280 pounds reasonably close to the surface of the snow. Without them I'd flounder like a bull moose in snow often waist deep.

With grub, axe, tea pail and a string of beaver traps I set out to test the white man's God. My breath froze as it left my mouth. As I increased my pace to an easy lope, I could quite well have resembled the ancient railway steam engine barrelling its way through the frosty air.

Cold temperatures posed no problem for me. I've lived in the north long enough to know how to dress. Pay attention to your feet. That's the first thing you learn. Mine were snug and warm in heavy woollen socks, moccasins and rubbers. Dry socks, that's the secret of survival in the north many times. Keep your feet warm and you'll be all right. Experienced hunters and trappers carry extra socks so they'll always have dry feet.

I was well up the trail before the sun nudged its way into a low arch across the southern sky. Daylight hours were few. By four o'clock in the afternoon the sun would lose its grip on the westward side of the hills and another cold, dark night would blanket the north.

I'd walked about eight miles before arriving at the area where I decided to start setting traps. Dropping my supplies on the ground I set about building a small fire, scooped up some snow in my tea pail and in a few minutes was nursing a hot mug of tea. I rested a short time and then picked up my axe.

Finding beaver runs (passages beavers use to come and go from their houses) isn't easy. Usually I had a dog trained to do this for me. I had one dog who could sniff out a run through six feet of snow. I don't know how he did it, but he never missed. But right now I had no food to spare for a dog, so I figured out where the runs were in my own way.

The ice was one and a half feet thick at this spot and I had to work hard to get through it. Most people had an ice chisel, but I didn't. I had to bend my back to an axe. I was sweating by the time I broke through to the water.

Three traps were all I was going to set this time. Normally I would have set more, especially since I'd tramped eight miles. But why should I? I'd dotted my entire trapline with traps for the last month without catching a single animal. Was the white man's prayer going to change things? I doubted it. It was probably like another one of those white man promises. They come at the Indian from all directions but don't help him much.

Still, I'd be fair to the missionary. I'd test his God. I couldn't pass up the slim chance that his powerful sounding words might have some strength to them after all.

The sun hung low in the ice-crystaled sky by the time I'd completed my task. I was hungry. I pushed a few dry branches together at the edge of a small bush, touched a match to a piece of bark and thawed out my lunch. I'm a fast eater and it wasn't long before I was full of garlic sausage, cheese and bread. I washed it down with a couple of mugs of hot tea. Fifteen minutes later, after changing into dry socks, I was on my way home.

I arrived after dark.

The following day I set out in a different direction and set a few traps. The next day I went in yet another direction and set a few more. In all I set out about ten or twelve traps.

I was satisfied. I'd done what the missionary wanted. My part was finished. Nobody could say I wasn't trying to cooperate. I rested easy. Thanks to Marshall passing me that twenty-dollar bill, I had a small grubstake to fall back on until I got the answer from his God. If there was to be an answer.

Come morning, I started out to check my first string of traps. The spark of hope must still have been alight in me because I decided to pull my toboggan along just in case I had fur to bring home.

It was an important day for me. Not only as a man who needed furs for income, but it was an important day for me as a witch doctor as well. If Marshall's God was victorious, what of the witchcraft spirits I had promised to worship? They had come to me and made promises to me and fulfilled those promises. I, in turn, had made promises to them. Could I break off with them like a person would break a twig? Would their anger be aroused?

It was no longer a case of filling my grub box. It was a case of obeying the spirits.

But there was little danger. I was well acquainted with the power of witchcraft and there would be little chance of the missionary's high-sounding prayer having any effect on the spirits I embraced and served. The missionary used no roots, did not mix up any dope. There was no smoke or steam bath. It was too simple. It was just another white man's remedy and would not work on the Indian.

Nevertheless there was a glimmer of expectation as I chopped through the ice and pulled on the chain of the trap. Even before the trap broke surface I knew it was empty.

I could have wept.

Anger welled up inside me. Marshall's God was wrong. I'd been taken in by the strong words. I should have gone to see the witch doctor. The evil power of the curse haunted me as I looked down at the empty trap at my feet.

I felt like returning home without as much as checking the other two traps in the area. But the north had disciplined a stubborn determination in me and I tramped on.

I was drained, weary and heavy-hearted. There was no purpose or feeling in me as I chopped the next hole. Without any hesitation I grabbed the chain and pulled.

The hair on my neck bristled.

The chain resisted my efforts. I heaved. A beaver slid through the hole and onto the ice.

My emotions were pulled in two directions. What had happened? Had the curse suddenly been lifted from me? Had the white man's God answered Marshall's prayer or was it simply that my luck was back?

I moved on to my next trap. Up came another beaver. My three strings of traps set during the last few days yielded nine beavers.

By the time Marshall came by sometime later I had seventeen beavers skinned and on stretchers.

He eyed me as he stepped into the cabin. I thought he would jump up and down like a squirrel, but he didn't. He was as calm as if his God answered a prayer every day.

"How are things going, Barney?"

I motioned toward the beaver skins. "Not bad," I told him. "I got seventeen beaver."

The missionary showed little surprise.

"My luck is back," I said, heaving myself from my big chair and working my way past the fur stretchers to the stove. "I'll get you a slab of bannock and some tea."

"That would be nice, Barney."

We visited in silence for the space of a few minutes.

"God is powerful, eh, Barney?" The missionary seemed to be trying to take away any suggestion that luck had any part in my success at trapping again. I had to admit that there was a chance that he might be right. But who was to know? I'd play it safe and try to get along with Marshall's God and the spirits of witchcraft, too.

"But what about moose, Barney? Have you been able to get a moose for food?"

"That's a thing I don't understand," I told him, pushing the bannock across the table. "I can't get near a moose anymore. They take off before I get anywhere near them, even when I'm downwind. I think the curse is on my hunting, too."

The missionary removed his parka and squeezed up beside me at the table.

"Barney, next time you go hunting, put your shells in your hand and pray over them. Ask God to cover them with the blood of His Son, Jesus Christ. There's power in the Word of God and the blood of Jesus."

That didn't sound too strange to me. A man who helped teach me witchcraft told me once of a root that was very powerful. You take this root and mix up a dope. This dope you would put on a bullet. But you couldn't touch the dope or the bullet with your fingers. You had to poke the bullet into the gun with a stick or something. Then you would tell the spirits which person you wanted to kill. You would think

38

about that person and shoot. Distance made no difference. Many people died this way. The spirits are powerful. This method was used by the spirits to stop a person's heart.

This same man carried a little pouchful of this stuff with him for fourteen years. You could put a little of the dope on the end of a stick and point it at a person and that person would die. You wouldn't get blamed for anyone's death because there would not be any marks on the person. Some Indians carried this dope for protection like a person would carry a gun.

Well, I didn't have to wait long to test out this new scheme of Marshall's.

A man came along a few days later and said, "Barney, let's go moose hunting."

I went with him.

It would be an easy trip because he had a jeep. I grabbed an axe, knife, tea pail and a little grub and we were off.

"How's trapping these days, Barney?" the man asked as we drove along.

"Good." I added no details.

"I hear you had a dry spell a while back."

"My luck is back now," I said.

We arrived at an area where we thought we should try and pick up some moose tracks. After parking the jeep, my partner went one direction and I went the other. When I got into a bush I took out my shells and laid them in my hand as the missionary had instructed. I prayed as best I knew how, trying to remember the words he told me to say.

Within three hours I was back on that same spot. I had shot and gutted three moose. They were ready to be picked up with the jeep. It was no problem as my partner had a power saw and we cut a trail right to the moose.

I was beginning to think that maybe Marshall's God was real and that He had a lot of power. Things the missionary had told me about the Gospel were at the edge of my mind. They were starting to dig into my thinking a little bit.

What was I going to do now?

I didn't think it would be possible to serve Marshall's God and the spirits of witchcraft at the same time. Something seemed to tell me that it wouldn't work.

I would have to run my mind over these things carefully.

3

Fork in the Road

Even though I was a witch doctor and a drunkard, every time the white man's Gospel came across my pathway, it took a little while for me to push the thoughts out and get about my business of being a witch doctor.

The first time I ever heard that a person could accept the Lord into his heart was when a Cree evangelist came to a logging camp I was operating. It was north of Green Lake, Saskatchewan. That young fellow's name was Bill Jackson. He told the Gospel to me. I never let on to anybody what I heard, but the thoughts were poked away someplace in the back of my mind. I wanted them to stay there, but they came out once in a while all on their own.

I was living common-law at the time and I said to myself, "This isn't the right thing to do." Nobody ever told me. I didn't even know what the Christian regulations were about it. Something inside told me.

Now, along comes Marshall Calverley. Just by praying to his God the curse is taken from my traps and I have good success hunting again. "How can these things be?" I wonder. "How can this man pray

41

and things happen?

"I'm a human being like him. I'm an Indian, but I've got a heart just like his. My prayer could be as powerful as his prayer if I was to serve the white man's God. But maybe it isn't for an Indian like me, especially since I'm a witch doctor."

Night after night these thoughts flowed over my mind like a river in flood stage. There I lay in my cabin in the backwoods far from civilization with the spirit of witchcraft and the Spirit of Marshall's God wrestling in my heart.

The year was 1960.

Finally, one night as I lay on my cot, the thoughts of the Great God of heaven came over me. My mind was made up. Marshall's God was a good Spirit. He was powerful. He could break a witchcraft curse just by a man asking Him to. He didn't need to mix up dope, burn sweet grass, take a steam bath or be offered a gift of tobacco or print cloth. Nothing! It was free!

I got off my bed and knelt down beside it. Lifting my right hand toward heaven I said, "Lord, take my hand. I surrender my heart and life and soul to You, Lord. I promise to live for You."

Something happened in my life. I don't know how to put it, but the empty place was filled. It was like I had company in the cabin.

Ever since I gave my life to Jesus I've been happy. Anybody can be as happy as me. I am never lonesome anymore. The Lord is looking after me all the time. I see thousands of people and you can tell by the way they look and act that there is something missing from their lives. Many people are trying to find happiness from a bottle, like I did once, but they won't find it until they find the Lord as Savior. I love my Lord.

Now, God answers prayers for me like He does for Marshall. I remember one winter I bought a horse and took him by truck to my trapline. After hooking him to my toboggan I went about setting my traps. Suddenly as we were travelling along over the ice on the lake, he broke through. Just his head and neck were sticking out. I didn't know what to do. We were quite a few yards from shore and I thought maybe I could chop the ice free to the shore.

It was hopeless. After a half-hour I had to stop. I couldn't stand to see the horse suffer any longer. I would have to put him out of his misery.

My rifle was on the toboggan, which didn't go through the ice. I took two steps toward it and stopped. It came to my mind what my little daughter often said: "Daddy, there is nothing too hard for the Lord."

I took my hat off and tossed it on the ice. A lot of Christian Indians take their caps off even in forty-below weather when they pray. Even if they take a cup of water some of them take their hats off and thank the Lord for it. I said, "Lord, help me find some kind of way to get my horse out of this hole in the ice."

While I was still praying, there was a great splash and the next second the horse was lying beside me on the ice. How he jumped from that hole I have never figured out to this day. He came up like you would take a tea bag from a cup and lay it by the side. If that's not a miracle, I don't know what you call it. God sure looked after me.

A few months after I was saved I was worried because I didn't feel well. My heart was bothering me and I thought I might die soon and I had the little

43

kids, Hazel and Freddie, to took after. Next time I met Marshall I pulled him to the side, "I wonder if you could help me get a paper fixed up so you could be the one to say what happens to my kids if I should die. I want them to be in a place where they'll learn about Jesus."

"I'll look after that just like you say, Barney," he told me. I was sure glad.

Another time when God answered a prayer was when somebody wanted me to go to the hospital to see a lady who was dying. She was an Indian lady about thirty-five or so years old. As I got to the hospital the nurse said to me, "She will not live another twenty-four hours."

I went to her room. She was lying there with two tubes in her nose and two needles in each hand. Her eyes were closed.

I talked to her in Cree, but she never opened her eyes or talked back. As I took one hand she opened her eyes. "You're sick," I said. "I've come to pray for you."

She closed her eyes again.

I stood there and prayed for her. Then I told her I would be gone for four days as I had to go away on a preaching trip east of Saskatoon.

In four days I arrived back in town and went to visit her just as I had promised. She was sitting on her bed. The tubes and needles were gone. As I walked toward her she said, "Barney, your prayers are powerful."

"If you would serve the same God I serve, your prayers would be powerful, too," I told her.

"When you were here before, I could hear what you were saying," she said to me. "When you said you were going to come back in four days I figured I'd be in my grave. I thought I'd never see you in four days."

She looked quite well sitting there on her bed. It was hard to believe that she was so sick just a few days before.

"Well, I have to go away for six days this time," I told her, "as I have to preach in another place. When I come back I'll drop in and see you."

"I believe you this time," she told me. "I believe I'll be living in six days."

On my return I again went to see her. She was sitting on a chair by the bed doing a little sewing. She laughed and shook my hand. "Barney, I'm very pleased at how things are turning out. I'm feeling very good. Pretty soon I'm going home."

Another time I was asked to see an old Indian man in Buffalo Narrows in northern Saskatchewan. He was ninety-four years old. Edwin Heal, the Northern Canada Evangelical Mission missionary there, took me to the old man's place.

As I stepped into the little cabin I could see the old man sitting on a couch with a set of beads in his hand. As I looked at him and heard his name I remembered I knew him from time past.

"What are you doing with these?" I said, pointing to the beads.

"You see me?" he said, looking up into my face. "I'm old. I'm ninety-four. Pretty soon I'm going to die. I want to go to heaven."

"All right," I spoke, "if you want to go to heaven, I'll tell you how to get there. Put the beads in my hand."

He placed the rosary in my hand and I placed it on the table. I don't condemn another man's ways because I was the same myself. I pulled my chair against his couch and preached the Gospel to him in Cree. I told him many things about salvation and how to get to heaven. "The Bible says, 'Believe on the Lord Jesus Christ and thou shalt be saved' " I told him.

Do you know, while I was sitting there, all at once tears were coming from his eyes and running down his face. "Barney, how come nobody ever told me such things as you're telling me today?" he asked.

We talked together for a long time in the language of his birth.

"I'm telling you the truth from the Bible," I told him. "What I'm saying to you right now is coming from the Holy Word of God."

"Do you know," he said, "I've been a Justice of the Peace at Isle-a-la-Crosse for many years. I've been Justice of the Peace at Buffalo Narrows for many years as well. People thought so much of me that they even named an island after me. It's called Mackay Island. But here I am at ninety-four and nobody ever told me the true way to heaven until today. I don't understand how that could be."

So I sat there still longer and told him more of the Gospel. I explained how Jesus died on the cross to pay for our sins; how Jesus could forgive us of our sins if we repented and asked forgiveness; how we must come to God through Jesus and Him alone. "There is one God and one mediator between God and man, the Man Christ Jesus" I told him. He grasped every word as it came from my lips.

"I have to go now, to the place where I'm staying," I told him. I'm coming back to see you tomorrow and I'll bring you a Bible printed in syllabics. I want you to have it to keep." He told me he could read syllabics.

46

Next day I was back at his cabin. When he saw that I had the Bible, he reached out his hands toward me. "Barney, do you know," he said, "I almost never slept last night. I slept a little on towards the morning. I was thinking about all the things you told me."

"Look," I said, opening the Bible and pointing to different pages. "I've underlined a lot of places in the Bible so you can find them and read them for yourself."

I passed the Bible to him. "It's yours," I told him.

He struggled to his feet and shook my hand in a gnarled grasp.

As we started to pray together he said, "I want to put my trust in Jesus."

There on the couch, the old man turned his life over to the Savior. "If I don't see you again down here, Barney, I'll see you up in heaven." He drew the Bible close to himself.

I was able to go back to Buffalo Narrows some time later. But the old man had passed away a month before. I asked about him. "Well, when he was about to pass away," I was told, "the priest came to administer the last rites. The old man motioned the priest back. "It's not necessary to do that. I'm all right. I've put my faith in Jesus. He has saved my soul." He asked his wife to come and fix his pillows under his head. She did so and he settled back and passed away, just like that. I'm glad the Lord led me to him so he could hear the Gospel before it was too late.

Most people are happy that I've come to the Lord, but not all. I remember when I was night watchman at a sawmill up north. People had always stolen oil and lumber before I came. But when I was hired I kept a close watch on things and stopped all that stealing. Well, I stayed in a little shack right there and people started shooting at the shack when I was in there. I told the police, but they said nobody would do that. I showed them the bullet holes and the bullets that were in the walls. I tried to be honest as I was a Christian, but I quit that job because I thought it was not worth getting killed over. I try to be honest in all things.

You see, when I became a Christian I gave up the things of the world. I gave up worshipping spirits and witchcraft. Just recently a man came to me with a blanket, a new rifle and some fruit. "Here, Barney," he said. "I'll give you these things if you do some witchcraft for me so I can get a moose."

"No," I said to him. "I'm serving the Lord Jesus now. I don't do witchcraft anymore."

4

I Was Fed Like a Dog

I was born Bernard Opekokew in 1901.

When I was thirteen, arrangements were made to send me away to Duck Lake Industrial School so I could get a little education. Until then, I had never been to school. Even with that opportunity I only got to grade four. I guess the most outstanding thing that happened to me at that place was that my name was changed. My teacher couldn't pronounce "Opekokew," which in Cree means "making ashes," so he decided to call me Bernard Lacendre. That's why I have a French name even though I'm a full blooded Cree. Everybody just calls me Barney.

According to what my mother told me, I was born at Canoe Narrows, north of Meadow Lake, Saskatchewan. My father died when I was two years of age. Hard times started for me when my mother remarried, because my stepfather seemed to have an awful dislike for me. I got some terrible lickings from that man when I was a little child.

"You were scared of him," my mother told me. "You used to crawl under the bed and stay there all the while your stepfather was in the cabin. I used to toss food under the bed to you so you wouldn't go hungry.'' My mother fed me like I was a little dog.

I loved the summertime. I stayed outside almost all the time. Sometimes I never even went home for the night. Nobody seemed to care about me. I usually had berries to eat or something else I'd find. During the summer I don't think I ever spent a full day in the cabin for fear of getting a licking.

About that time my stepfather decided to take us out to a homestead about nine miles west of Duck Lake. There were no roads then, just wandering wagon trails. My time was spent roaming around the countryside with a little dog we had. Rain or shine I stayed away from the cabin and my stepfather's stick.

One bright sunny day I came across a haystack. I decided to sit in the sun at the edge of the stack and rest awhile. The dog curled up beside me and I ran my hand over his soft fur coat. It felt good to have a friend.

Well, I guess I fell asleep because the next thing I knew the sun was just leaning against the horizon. I figured it was a good place to spend the night so I dug a hole into the haystack and my dog and I settled down.

It was dark when the dog awoke me with his barking. I stuck my head out the hole and standing right there at the opening was a herd of cows. It really put a fear into me and I crouched back in the hole shaking. The dog got a little braver and barked loud enough to scare the cows away. We got back to sleep after a while. I was only five years old then.

When I awoke in the morning I was hungry, and as I was about a mile from the cabin I decided to take a chance on my stepfather being out working.

However, on the way something caught my attention and held me up for a while. A bunch of my stepfather's pigs were poking around at the edge of the lake. I had been interested for some time to see whether pigs could swim the same as dogs. This was a good time to test it out I thought. The lake came to a long point right at that spot with a narrow strip of water right where the pigs were eating. I found a good, big stick and started chasing them. It took a little effort, but I finally managed to get them into the water and they headed for the other side. They could swim, all right. I was satisfied.

I struck off for the cabin, but didn't mention to my mother about the pigs being across the water. Maybe there was reason for my stepfather using his stick sometimes.

All day long I had to be doing something while I was outside. I remember this one day I got a rope around the neck of a steer. I tried to get on his back but couldn't make it, so I tied a piece of wood to the end of the rope and let him pull that around so he'd get used to hauling something. Finally I got the idea that I should get some more rope and hook him to an old cutter that was sitting in the yard. He didn't seem to mind pulling the cutter, so I decided to get in and enjoy a ride. My sister thought she should get in on the excitement and joined me. We didn't go any particular place because we had no way of steering the animal. He just more or less wandered around wherever he wanted to. Our yelling sometimes speeded up the process a bit. The steer naturally became quite important to us now that he added to our adventures. So we thought he was worthy of a name. We called him Pete.

Well, one day my stepbrother wanted to have a ride

with us. He was quite small and wrapped in a lace bag like a papoose. I guess Pete had the idea that we were going to keep adding more passengers all the time, so he decided he would put a stop to it. He took off as hard and fast as he could go.

My sister and I jumped out, but my little stepbrother was still in the cutter as it bounced up and down across the field and finally turned over and over. All the while my sister was crying and chasing after Pete.

When we got to where my little stepbrother had been dumped out on the ground, he didn't even seem to be hurt. We looked him over, decided we wouldn't have any more rides that day, unhooked Pete and headed back to the cabin.

I can still remember when I was six years of age how people had great respect for the priest whenever he made his rounds in the district. I saw how people looked up to him and spoke with great respect. Even at that age I thought how wonderful it would be if when I was older people would respect me like that.

These thoughts would keep coming to my mind. One day while I was down by my stepfather's corrals these things were in my mind again. I knelt down right there on the ground and asked God to make me a priest when I grew up. I wanted to be an important person in the community. I didn't know how to pray, but these thoughts were going up to God as I said, "Hail, Mary, Mother of God," and the rest of the prayer that I had heard people say.

The thought of being someone important was never far from my mind. I remember so well one day when I was out trapping. I was nineteen then. As I was tramping over the muskeg, skirting the shore of a lake, I came upon a little tamerac tree. I laid my supplies on the ground and knelt by that little tree. "God," I said, "make me into a preacher." Well, it took fifty years, but God made me into a preacher, all right.

When I was eight years old we moved again to a ranch near Leask, Saskatchewan. Shortly after the move my mother went for a month's stay at Green Lake. At the end of that time my stepfather announced, "We're going overland to get Mother. We'll start tomorrow."

My stepfather and I got along a little better by then, as I was able to do a few useful jobs for him. We were excited as we packed some grub for the trip. There were my stepfather, my two stepbrothers and me. We were taking the wagon and horses.

We dropped my two stepbrothers off near Leoville so they could dig seneca roots. We left some food with them and travelled on. If they had good luck in getting roots it would add to the family income.

When we arrived at the place where the river enters the south end of Green Lake we found the water at flood level. It was no use trying to take the wagon through the deep water. We were still eighteen miles from the settlement of Green Lake and my stepfather didn't know what to do. Finally he turned to me.

"You stay here with some of the horses and the wagon. I'll take one horse and swim across the river and go on to Green Lake. I'll come back for you in a few days."

"I don't want to stay here in the wilderness all by myself," I told him. Tears started down my cheeks. "Can't I go too?"

"Somebody has to stay with the horses and

53

wagon," he said without feeling. "You'll be all right."

I didn't look forward to the morning, but it came and I watched my stepfather take his clothes off and tie them to the saddle of the horse and lead it out into the river. When they were in deep water he grabbed the horse's tail so the horse could pull him across as it swam. Once on the other side he took his dry clothes from the saddle, pulled them on, jumped into the saddle and was gone.

I sat by the riverside crying.

My small frame was still heaving with sobs as I wandered back to the wagon a short time later. I didn't know what to do. It was wilderness—just bush except for the small clearing at the edge of the river where the horses grazed. They were hobbled. Anyway, they'd stay in the clearing where there was grass to eat.

Climbing into the wagon I poked around under a blanket to see what my stepfather had left me for grub. There was some bannock, butter and a sawed-off shot gun. There was also a case of whiskey, but at the time I didn't know what it was.

There was a big hill just off to the west of where I was camped. The sun would settle behind it at about four in the afternoon. That was the time I set for going to bed. I'd crawl into the wagon, get under the blanket and pull it right up over my head. When I was all covered I'd pull the loaded shot gun close to me and go to sleep. My lonesome day would start next morning when the sun got up. The sun was my light, my clock and my companion for the next five days.

My days were spent walking around in the clearing. I kept my eyes on the horses as my stepfather had instructed, but they gave me no cause for concern. I soon adjusted to my situation, because even though I was only eight years old I'd spent a lot of time alone in the bush. I didn't know how long my bannock had to last me, so I ate a chunk of it whenever I needed to take the edge off my hunger. Whenever I was thirsty I went to the river for a drink.

It was on the afternoon of the fifth day that I thought I heard a noise in the bush. I had already gone to bed. Poking my head out of the blanket, I listened. It sounded like people hollering off in the distance. I threw the blanket off and jumped up. It was people hollering my name. I stuck the shot gun into the air and pulled the trigger. The blast of the recoil almost kicked me out of the wagon.

When the voices got a little closer I fired another shot so they'd know where I was.

Pretty soon my stepfather, little stepsister, mother and uncle emerged from the bush. They had come overland. I was so happy I wept.

I had a hard life pretty well from the day I was born. In the summertime I forged for myself and ate a lot of berries and things. I guess I figured I owed myself a little pleasure once in a while, so came up with a lot of funny schemes. One day when I was coming back from my stepsister's place, I saw a big hole in the side of a hill. I thought I'd go home and tell my stepfather I saw a big, dark animal go into that hole. I think I did some of these things to get my stepfather's mind off beating me.

I started talking as soon as I burst through the door.

"I saw a big, dark animal go into a hole," I yelled excitedly. "It was a great big thing." I extended my arms to emphasize my point.

"Where?" my stepfather hollered.

"It was a big hole on the side of that hill on the way

55

to Grandpa's place. I saw the animal. It was terrible big.'' I was pleased my story was being accepted so readily.

My stepfather sent word to my uncle, grabbed a pick and shovel and pushed me out the door. ''Come on, show us.'' He was almost tramping on my heels in the excitement. He probably thought it was a bear, which would mean grease, fur and meat.

My uncle caught up to us before we got to the hole and we all arrived puffing and panting.

''All right, let's start digging,'' instructed my stepfather. They took turns with the pick and shovel until they'd worked their way right to the end of the tunnel. All the while I was standing back watching.

Finally they stepped back, sweating profusely.

''I guess he must have gone before we got here,'' put in my uncle, pulling his sleeve across the sweat dripping from his chin.

They shook their heads and we started back home.

When we got home I dragged a pig trough down to the lake, intending to paddle across the lake in it. After a few unsuccessful attempts I gave up that plan for a better one. I had noticed my folks leaving for town in the wagon, so I went to the cabin and got the shot gun. I was under strict orders not to use it, but the opportunity seemed too good to pass.

I had noticed some ducks hanging around our side of the lake and determined to try my luck. My first blast lifted a duck out of the air. Another duck was flying low over the water and I dropped him as well, but he fell in the water and I had no way of bringing him to shore.

When my folks got home they said, ''Where did you get that duck?''

''I found him,'' I lied.

I was so proud of getting him that I couldn't resist taking him home.

With that experience behind me, I hooked up Pete and he wandered down on a point of land between two lakes. I had often gone there because there were thousands of garter snakes on the rocks. The rocks were so covered with snakes that you could hardly tell the rocks were there. I used to take a stone and smash the snakes with it. On this particular day when I was killing snakes something came through the air and hit me right beside my eye. It was like the white of an egg. There were some birds flying around there at the time. I still remember that to this day—though it was seventy years ago.

5

Two Arson Attempts

I'm really a self-taught man. Most things I know were picked up back in the bush. Until I found God I never travelled more than a few hundred miles in any direction from where I was born. After the Lord came into my life He sent me far and wide to places of which I had only dreamed.

I was nine years old when my folks decided I should have a little education. There was no school near where we lived, so plans were made for another Indian to look after me and send me to school. It was four years later that the big day arrived. I was put in the Duck Lake Industrial School. It was a big place run by priests and nuns. They had a farm in connection with the school and boys' and girls' dormitories.

I had been living outdoors too long to fit into such a situation, and things didn't go all that well. After grade four they decided to make a farmer out of me and put me in charge of the horses and cattle. Even though I had a great love for horses I didn't want to stay there.

The First World War came along and as I was big

for my age, I thought I could lie and get into the army. This didn't work out either, because the priest would cut pictures out of the paper of buildings that had been destroyed in the war. "Look, Barney, if you'd been in that building, you'd be dead right now. Don't go. Stay here."

That priest sure liked me a lot. He kept coaxing me to stay.

I hated that place. I would sit down sometimes and try and think of a way to get out of there. Finally I decided that the best way to do it would be to burn the place down. They don't know to this day that I was the one who tried to do that.

As I looked the situation over I found a board broken out of one wall on the outside of a building. It was one of the dorms, but I thought everyone would get out anyway.

It was no problem for me to get in the storage shed and get some gas that they used in the gas lamps. There was no electricity at the school then.

With my plan all organized I went to bed.

When I was sure everyone was asleep, I crept out of my bunk and slipped down the dark stairs. Keeping close to the side of the building, I moved to the spot where I had noticed the broken board. Throwing in the gasoline I stepped back and tossed a match at it. It burst into a ball of flame.

In a matter of seconds I was back in bed.

I lay there with a picture in my mind's eye of the flames creeping up the side of the very building in which I was sleeping. In a minute I'd pretend I'd just woke up and discovered the fire. I was all ready to holler, "Fire," when somebody beat me to it.

"Fire! Fire!"

The yells rang down the corridor.

"Everybody out."

I tumbled out of bed with the rest of the boys and tried to act as surprised as they were. The men were racing around battling the fire by every means imaginable. I was sure I'd be on my way home before the day was out.

But this was not to be. The fire was extinguished in short order and we were sent back to bed.

There were 35-40 boys at the school and the priests tried desperately to find the one who started that fire. They finally came to the conclusion that it was a certain boy. I kept my mouth shut through the whole ordeal.

The boy was called to face the charges.

"We'll have to send you away to another school," they told the youngster in their stern manner.

"B-But I didn't do it," protested the boy. "I was sleeping. I woke up when everybody was hollering, 'Fire!' "

"You're always getting into trouble, so you must have had something to do with it." Their minds were made up. I guess in the minds of the rest of the school staff, the priests had performed their job well. I was the only one who knew the truth and I wasn't going to let anyone else in on the secret.

The condemned youngster was shipped off to another school and ended up receiving a really good education. I kind of wished I'd been caught in the act and been the one condemned, so I could have gotten a better education.

I still hated that school enough to try to burn it down a second time.

This time I did a little more planning.

As I went about my job I kept my eyes open for a good place to start my next fire. It wasn't long before

I found the perfect place. Under one of the stairwells I found a catch-all place for papers and junk. A little coal oil and a match should put me on the road home.

This time I waited for a nice, warm day. Everyone was outside enjoying the beautiful weather. I ambled around the corner of a building and in no time was inside.

Making sure no one was around, I poured a can of coal oil on the junk and touched a match to it. Racing outside, I joined the rest of the youngsters, making sure I was heard as I yelled and squealed with the boys. I had a good alibi. I was playing, as all could plainly see.

"Fire! Fire!"

Men with hoses and buckets seemed to appear out of nowhere.

"There goes my fire again," I thought.

I was right. They put it out.

They never found out who started that fire. But they must have wondered if they'd sent the right fellow off to that other school after the first fire.

For the moment I had run out of ideas of how best to get away from the school.

There were a lot of boys who didn't like going to school and every once in a while some would take off and run away. I don't know why I never took off, but I think I realized that my folks would ship me right back and I'd get punished on top of it.

Anyway, I was a big fellow and was always picked to go after these runaways. One time two fellows took off. We caught one right away, but the second one got away. We got a horse and rig and took up the search. His trail led us fifteen miles from the school. We finally had to leave the rig and track him through bush. I could sure run in those days and I stayed right behind this fellow. At one point he ducked behind a tree stump. He took his boots off, and when I came up he threw them at my head. I caught him anyway and half dragged him back to the rig.

It was at that school that I took the only beating of my life. It happened one morning when we were all in the washroom. My towel had disappeared.

"You've got my towel," I hollered at a fellow who had a towel that looked like mine. I grabbed it and held on.

"This is mine," protested the youngster, jerking the other end of the towel violently.

I didn't want any explanations and gave him a swift kick to express my thoughts. He obliged me with two black eyes.

That day as I stood humiliated before the rest of the fellows, I decided I would never again take a beating as long as I lived. It turned out to be true. That was my last licking. I practised boxing every chance I got.

This was a religious school, but we weren't allowed to read the Bible. If, by chance, they let us read it, they would always tell us what to believe. It was their own Bible and different from the one I use now. They didn't tell us about a person needing a Savior to take his sins away. They told us that we had to pay for our sins—but the Bible tells us that Jesus died on the cross for our sins. He paid the price for our sins. We just have to repent and believe. I'm so thankful I found the Lord. I want to live a good Christian life and follow God's will every day of my life.

Well, that fight over the towel didn't help my reputation much and before I knew it I was standing before the priest.

"Barney, what is the matter with you?" He always

63

spoke gently to me because he liked me and had great plans for my life. "Don't you like it at the school, Barney?"

I shook my head. I didn't want to speak out against his authority.

"I was thinking," he continued, pointing to a chair by his sturdy desk, "if you stay on until you're about nineteen or twenty, I could set you up on a little farm of your own. You know all about cattle and horses, Barney."

I slid onto the hardwood chair without speaking.

"Barney, I know of a girl you could marry and I would get you in the Duck Lake reserve. I'll give you a team of horses and everything."

He rose from behind the desk and stood beside me, expectantly awaiting my reply.

I shook my head again. "I don't think so," I said, hardly above a whisper.

"Why are you acting this way, Barney?" His voice took on a stern edge. "I've been good to you."

"I don't like the school." I offered the words fearfully. "I want to go home."

The priest shook his head and sat down sadly. He didn't give me permission to go home, and so I was no better off. It wasn't until a short time later, when he found out I was sneaking over to the girls' dorm, that things came to a head.

"Barney, I think I'd better let you go home," he said flatly. "Next thing I know, you'll be after the nuns." I think he was jealous of me to tell you the truth.

So arrangements were made to send me home. I was eighteen at the time and had been at the school for five years.

The priest took me to the railway station, bought

me a ticket, gave me a little spending money and watched me get on the train. The train would take me to Big River. From there I would strike off overland to Green Lake where my folks lived.

There was a great uproar when I walked into our house.

"Barney is home! Barney is home!" hollered my stepfather. You see, my stepfather was good to me now that I'd grown up. I was able to do a man's work alongside of him and he became proud of me.

"We'll have a celebration tonight," he yelled above the commotion. "We'll have a big dance."

It was a great celebration, all right. Horse rigs were drawn up all over the yard. Friends came for miles around and my mother prepared a big feast.

That was the end of my school days.

6

Six Shells—Seven Caribou

I was nineteen now, and by my stepfather's standards old enough to carry a rifle. I'd been using a firearm of some sort ever since I was old enough to hold a gun to my shoulder, but in an undercover kind of way in order to save myself a beating. My main trouble was that when I was sent home from school I didn't have enough money to buy a rifle of my own. However, a priest from Green Lake took a liking to me and used to loan me his.

My life centered around that gun. I would hunt from morning until night. I loved being alone and free. I loved the bush country. Day after day I trudged across muskeg, around lakes, through tangled underbrush, always with my eyes peeled for some moving creature.

On one such trek I came upon a moose and wounded him. He took off, leaving blood on the branches of the trees as he went. Every time he stopped he left a patch of blood on the ground. As I approached, he would get up and run a short distance. Whenever I came upon a branch with blood on it I would break it off and shove it in my pocket. If

I didn't get the moose, at least I wanted to have evidence to show people that I had really wounded one.

By the time I got home, that was all I had—a bunch of bloody branches. I never did get the moose.

Come spring, my luck changed. Early March found me on the trail of another moose. This one was a huge bull moose. I was downwind and worked myself quietly into a good position for a shot. He was unaware of my presence. I raised the rifle and took my time setting his neck between the sights. Gently I squeezed the trigger. The bullet slammed into him, but he never budged. A second quick shot dropped him.

I moved up cautiously, my rifle trained on his head. I'd heard too many tales of hunters who had been slashed by moose that were supposedly dead.

Standing over him I saw a sight that I was to see many times in the north. The moose was almost completely covered with wood ticks. It was almost impossible to see any of his hair. There were thousands of ticks. Big ones.

While I was standing there the moose moved a bit. I pumped another shot into him. I remember I fired fourteen shots into that moose. Even if he moved a leg I shot him. I wanted to make sure I got this fellow.

He was my first moose.

I bled the moose with real pride in my heart. Then I skinned and gutted him and went home. To this day I remember how I felt. I was so proud I could hardly talk to my mother and stepfather for quite a while. But it wore off as I shot other moose, and I don't mind saying that I became a fairly good shot. We always had meat on the table and hides to make jackets and moccasins. I've shot moose, caribou, elk and bear; lots of them.

I was known to be one of the best hunters in the country. I could stick nails in a tree and hammer them in with .22 bullets. Today I can hardly hit the tree. At seventy-eight years of age my eyesight is starting to go. But I still go hunting and trapping and get the odd moose as well.

During those early years I stayed around home for a while, but I needed a job so I went to work for a man named Everest Beaulac, a farmer who lived near Leask, Saskatchewan. I worked for him for about ten years and he asked me to stay on.

Instead, I went back to hunting and guiding. I had a few cabins and tents spaced out along my trapline and right from the beginning I had no shortage of hunters to guide for. In those days hunters were allowed two caribou for each license. Sometimes the hunters would stay in the cabin and I would go out and get their big game. I found it better than having them wandering around scaring the animals. Even to this day American hunters look me up and want me to guide for them. I'm old now, but I can't seem to let my trapline go. It's a part of me. I can't seem to just settle back in my old age.

My time won't be long, I guess, but I'm ready to die. If somebody said to me, "You'll be dead in five minutes," I'd just prepare myself to be dead. I know that I'm a child of God. I've put my trust in Jesus. I have no fear, as I'm on my way to heaven. I'm a child of the family of God.

I couldn't have said that back in the 1950s. I was an outlaw then. I had an emptiness in my life that I didn't know how to fill. When I found Christ as my Savior I knew what I had been looking for. Nobody can tell me the kind of life there is out in the world of sin. I was the devil's number one angel. Now I'm walking with God.

I remember one time I had on my white hunting jacket. It was made out of a Hudson's Bay blanket by my mother. If I was standing in the snow it was almost impossible to see where I was. So this time when I was out hunting I saw some caribou off in the distance. They didn't know I was there, and I was downwind, so I just stood still. On they came in single file. There were seven of them, with the buck at the lead. It was almost as though I was invisible. They kept coming directly toward me.

When the big buck was about thirty feet from me he stopped short and sniffed the air. He knew something was wrong. His uneasiness was picked up by the other caribou. I knew I had only a second or two in which to act.

I had six shells in the magazine of my 30-30 and in one motion I lifted the rifle and pumped the bullets into the herd. They were startled and for that brief few seconds didn't know which way to turn. When my rifle was empty there were seven caribou on the ground.

Don't ask me what happened. The only thing possible is that I got two caribou with one bullet. That is the one and only time that happened in all my years of hunting.

As I was gutting the caribou I noticed through the corner of my eye that one of them, a little to the side of the rest, was starting to move. By the time I got to where he was, he was on his feet and away.

I started after him. He ran a short distance and lay down, leaving a patch of blood. When I was almost on him, he was up and away. I knew that it was only a matter of time before he would bleed to death, so I kept after him. Finally, after following him for a long while, I came right up to him and he never moved. I was sure he was dead.

Suddenly, I was caught unawares. Before I could make a move, he was up and charging me. I grabbed my rifle and swung it with all my might. I hit the horns just before they would have pierced me. They broke off, taking part of the skull with them. The big buck landed on my feet, dead.

I was tired by the time I got back to the cabin, so just directed the men where to go to pick up the caribou. But I found my rest was short-lived. Two men, a father and son from Biggar, Saskatchewan, stopped by my cabin. They had licenses for caribou and wanted to get theirs that day.

I pulled on dry socks, poured a cup of tea from the pot, broke off a slab of bannock and kicked the door open. I got their four caribou and was back at the cabin before dark.

The father motioned me to one side.

"Look," he said in a secretive voice. "How about getting me one or two extra caribou? I've got a friend back home who would like one."

I shook my head.

"Come on, Barney," persisted the father. "I'll make it worth your while." He patted the wallet outlined in his hip pocket.

"It's illegal," I told him. "I'm a licensed guide. I can't lose my reputation."

The old man scoffed and reached for his parka.

"I'll get one for myself," he said, grabbing his rifle. "It didn't take you long to get those."

"Look," I warned him sternly, emphasizing my point with the end of my finger. "It's starting to snow out there and the wind is picking up. You'll get lost in no time. I know what I'm talking about."

He paid me no heed and I was in no mood to argue with him.

"Tell your dad to come back," I said to the son. "He won't see a landmark out there in a few minutes and darkness is going to be on him in an hour."

"Dad, come back," hollered the son, jerking the door open and shouting into the gathering storm. "Barney said it's dangerous for you."

"I'm all right. I'll just circle around here a bit. I'll keep the cabin in sight." He threw the words over his shoulder and was lost to the falling snow.

It wasn't long before we could hear the blasts of snow striking the window as the wind picked up. I half expected the old man to stumble through the door at any minute, but he didn't.

"What are we going to do about him?" The son was worried.

I shrugged my shoulders as if there was no need for concern. But I knew the father was already lost and couldn't hope to see a caribou in this storm.

"Let's get those caribou that you shot a while ago," suggested the youngster. "If Dad sees them he'll be satisfied."

I'd intended to leave the caribou out until morning before bringing them in, but they weren't far off and it would ease the young fellow's mind if we were doing something.

We'd just nicely got the caribou back to the cabin when the storm struck with new fury. Loose boards on the roof of the cabin creaked and rattled. Snow sifted through, leaving wet patches here and there on the floor.

"Barney, look, we've got to do something about my

72

dad. It's bad out there."

I looked at the young fellow. He was about twenty years of age. A nice clean-cut sort of guy. I knew there was no use putting him off. I also knew there was little point in hunting for a man in a virtual whiteout.

"All right, come on," I said, grabbing my parka and pulling the hood over my head. I shoved some dry socks, food and shells into a bag, lifted the coal oil lantern off the wire dangling from the ceiling, and motioned the youngster out the door.

As soon as we stepped into the face of the blizzard I knew it was going to be a long night.

"We'll strike north about two miles and make a big circle," I hollered above the wind. "He'll be inside that area somewhere, I think."

The lantern kept blowing out because of the wind and it was almost impossible to get a match going long enough to relight it. The young fellow was half running, trying to keep up with me. Every little while he grabbed my arm.

"Barney, we're lost. We're lost. Let's head back to the cabin."

I jerked myself free from his grasp.

"Leave me alone," I shouted. "I know how to travel in the bush. Just keep your ears open and follow me."

Every little while I'd stop and fire a shot into the air and listen for an answering shot from the old man. It never came.

It was 2:00 a.m. when we completed our circle and stood on the spot from which we started. The old man had not returned to the cabin, which did not surprise me in the least. I picked up a few more shells at the cabin, but I was running low. From now on I'd use them sparingly if we went out again.

The youngster was shaken, tired and desperate. He pulled at my arm. "What about it, Barney? Are we going to find Dad?"

"Well, I guess he's lost all right," I said simply. "Maybe in daylight he'll find his way out." I was blunt, but I'd warned the old man.

"We can't wait and see," protested the youngster. "He might freeze to death in the meantime."

I pushed wood into the stove and set the tea pail over the flames. "I've done about all I can do," I told the boy. "If the storm lets up a bit I'll go out again."

"Barney, we've got to get a search party out after Dad." He paced about in the semi-darkness of the cabin; sitting for a few seconds, then jumping to his feet.

"Where can we get men, Barney? We've got to get help. Dad may be lying out there freezing."

I guess I knew how the youngster felt. Wearily I pulled on my parka. "I'll go to Green Lake and round up some men." I was tired, but I couldn't sleep with the old man out there. Anyway, the boy wouldn't let me.

"B-But that's nine miles away," shouted the youth as I opened the door.

"That's where the men are," I said bluntly, bracing myself into the storm.

I was able to rouse six men from their beds and we got a team of horses and a sleigh, so we saved time coming back to the cabin.

There would be no sleep for me until the job was done because none of the men knew the area like I did. I'd have to organize the plan of search and go with it.

We put on dry socks and packed grub.

Once out in the general area I called the men about me.

"Now, listen," I had to shout above the wind. "I think the old man headed that way." I pointed into the whiteness. "I want two men to go in that direction. I want two more men to go two miles farther north and strike out in a circle and I want you other two men to go still farther two miles and make your circle."

They chatted together for a minute and paired off.

"I'll fork off in another direction," I said. "If anybody finds the old man, fire two shots. The others will hear them and fire two shots until the message gets back to me."

We separated into the storm.

My instinct seemed to tell me which way I should go and I hit off straight into the bush. After covering about a mile and a half I came out on open muskeg. Scrub spruce about three feet high dotted the area. The storm was easing up slightly and I could see about a hundred yards now. I hadn't searched the white landscape long before I saw a dim form far up ahead of me. I increased my pace. Sure enough, it was the old man, still plodding along in the wrong direction.

"Hey," I hollered. "Stop!"

He kept moving. The wind carried my words away before they reached him. It was unbelievable that the old man should still be walking after all those hours.

I put my rifle in the air and pumped off two quick shots.

The old man stopped as quickly as if his body had absorbed the bullets.

The rifle reports from the others drifted over like

echoes. They knew the hunter had been found.

But for the tiredness I would have laughed at the sight of the old man stumbling back through the deep snow toward me. He clutched onto my arm like a dying man.

"Barney, B-Barney," he gasped, "I've been walking all night." He started to cry. I hadn't seen a grown man cry before. Frost covered his eyebrows, whiskered face and parka hood. He was some sight.

I guided him to the edge of the bush and sat him on a felled tree. "Here, eat," I said, pushing some bannock toward him from my grub bag.

He shook his head.

Pumping a shell from the chamber of his rifle, he laid it on his mitt.

"See this?"

I nodded.

"It's the last one I had. If I hadn't found the cabin by nightfall tonight, I was going to put it between my eyes."

He meant it, all right. I could see it written on his face and in his eyes. You don't fool around in the north. It's cruel. You've got to know its ways and respect it.

I pulled dry socks from the pocket of my parka and told him to put them on. Dry socks do something for the whole body.

Again he shook his head.

"All right, let's get back to camp, then," I told him. The old man stayed right at my heels like a dog.

On the way we had to cross a creek. It was running swift under the ice at one point and was the next thing to open water. The old fellow broke the thin ice with the heel of his boot and dropped to his knees. I just stood there and marvelled at how long he drank. I guess he'd been eating snow, which only gives you more thirst.

When we came into sight of the cabin, I could see the son standing outside watching. When he saw his dad coming he ran to meet him. As they came together it was just like a dam broke. Boy, did that young fellow cry! I don't know if crying runs in the family, but he was sure glad to see his dad alive.

While we had the horses at the cabin, they loaded up the caribou meat and got ready to go to Green Lake. The old man and his son could hardly wait to get back to civilization. Before he left he handed me the money for getting his caribou. He gave me twenty dollars, which was five dollars for each caribou. Then he pulled me to the side.

"Barney, I want to thank you for finding me out there. I wish I could give you some more money to make it up to you, but this is all I've got."

I told him it was all right.

He touched my arm. There was something like an embarrassed look plastered on his tired, old face.

"I was going to give you forty dollars, Barney, but I know you're a proud man. I didn't know how to go about it." He looked over at the others as if they would have the words he was searching for. "I had a little paper leaflet in my pocket and I put the forty dollars in there. I was going to hand the leaflet to you as we were leaving and you'd find the money after." He cleared his throat. "You know, when I was lost in the storm, I got kind of scared and was trying to start a fire. There was no bark or twigs around and I remembered I had this leaflet. I used that to try to start a fire, but I forgot about the money. I burned the money, Barney. I'm sorry."

I didn't want to laugh at the old man, but I laugh at

it now. I guess he was sure glad to get back to Biggar.

Attacked by a Bear

I was about twenty years old the winter I went trapping east of Smoothstone Lake. Even at that early age I loved to be alone in the backwoods. I was my own boss and I could come and go as I pleased. Muskrat fur was at its prime between November and April and I stayed through the whole season.

In the spring I took my catch of furs to the Hudson's Bay store in Green Lake and paid off my debts. They had staked me my supplies for the winter: grub, shells, traps and clothes. When the manager finished his figuring, I was about broke. But I'd had a good winter. What more could you ask?

Rather than bum around the settlement I decided the best thing would be to go to my uncle, Baptiste Merasty. He had a few head of cattle and a stopping-off place at Sled Lake. People on long trips through that part of the country would lay over a day or two to rest their horses. Uncle Baptiste was glad of my help around the place and my dog Spooney enjoyed the excitement of people coming and going.

Uncle Baptiste was a great man for trapping bear. I don't know why he was like that. It was kind of a hobby, I think. Well, this one time he caught a bear, but it tore the chain loose and took off with the trap dangling from its foot. Now, a bear trap is a big and expensive thing and my uncle wanted it back. He knew Spooney was good at tracking and he rushed over to where I was tending stock.

"Barney, quick, get hold of Spooney," he shouted, though I was standing next to him. "I want you to track a bear for me. I don't care about the bear, but I want my trap back."

"I'll try and get the bear, too," I told my uncle. I whistled and Spooney appeared at my side. "After all," I continued, "we don't want to pass up thirty-five to forty dollars for the hide, do we?"

Picking up my rifle from the cabin and grabbing a handful of shells from the box, I headed toward the bush.

"Where are you going, Barney?"

It was my cousin who was stopping over for a while.

"Come on," I hollered, "you'll find out."

Tying a rope to the dog's neck we led him all over the area. Suddenly he picked up something. "Go get him, boy," I said, turning him loose.

Spooney took off, with us running hard behind him. Pretty soon the dog started barking and I knew he'd caught up to the bear.

"There he is," I shouted to my cousin. "Look there, through the scrub spruce."

We both got a shot off but missed.

The bear was mad. The trap hampered him and every time the dog got near enough to nip him, he'd turn around and swing at Spooney. This gave us time to get closer. All at once the trap flew to the side. It had cut right through the bear's foot. The roar of the animal sent shivers up our spines.

I was getting closer all the time. My cousin stopped
and picked up the trap, but I kept running. The dog
nipped the bear again and as it swung around it saw
me right there.

I was too close.

I jerked my rifle up, intending to aim. I was too late.
The big fellow was in the air heading toward me. The
bloody stump of one foot dripped blood. His lips
curled back exposing yellow teeth.

Pointing the rifle, I pulled the trigger.

The bullet tore into the bear at point-blank range.
He fell dead against my leg. He was big, about
500-600 pounds.

We skinned him for his hide. In hard times we
would have used his meat and grease as well.

That night my uncle gave me a few drinks. I guess
it was in payment for the good job I'd done
concerning the bear. Anyway, I didn't get drunk. I
knew what was going on around me all the time. Yet
when I was ready to leave for the south a day or two
later he pulled me to the side.

"Don't forget, you've got to leave Spooney here
with me," he said.

"What do you mean?" I asked him.

"When you were drunk the other night you gave
Spooney to me," he told me.

I knew that was wrong.

"He's my dog. I didn't give him to you."

"Yes, you did," he said. "You gave him to me."

Well, I gave him Spooney. If he said I told him that,
I would obey him.

I felt sorry leaving Spooney there. He watched me
as I got into my canoe and started across the lake. He
just stood on the shore. He didn't bark or make a
fuss. He just watched me with sad eyes.

It was some time later when I found out what happened to Spooney. My cousin told me.

"You know, when you left that day," he said, "you took off your old moccasins and socks and threw them on the shore. Spooney gathered them up and put them in one place. Then he lay by them. He wouldn't come to the cabin to eat or anything. After two days when I looked for him at that spot, he was gone. I looked all around but there was no sight of him. I happened to look out on the lake and there he was, swimming in the direction you had gone. I got my boat right away and started after him, but by the time I'd paddled to where he was he'd just gone under. I'm sorry about that, Barney."

"It's not your fault," I said to my cousin.

"Baptiste lied, you know, about you giving Spooney to him," put in my cousin. "He wanted Spooney because he was a good tracker."

This is the same dog who caught three fox in one day. One of them was pretty tough for him to get, but I got close enough to get a shot in to help him out.

Lots of times he would chase a fox into a den and dig him out. One day he chased two cross fox and one red fox into a hole and got them all. That's how good he was.

I remember one time when we were really hard up. I needed a few fox furs to trade at the Hudson's Bay store for food, so I took Spooney on a fox hunt. We travelled two or three miles before he picked up a scent. Then away he went, with me after him.

Spooney tracked the fox to a den and I gave him a hand digging it out. You know, we found two red fox in there. They were worth eight dollars apiece in those days. That was a lot of money.

Another time we were tracking a fox past my brother Joe's cabin. He was giving another fellow a haircut out on the door step. They hollered at me as we approached.

"Come on in for a visit, Barney."

"Not this time," I yelled back. "I'm after a fox."

Joe laughed.

"How are you going to catch a fox? You haven't got any traps."

"I don't need traps," I told him. "I've got Spooney."

Well, the fox ran right up to the hole of a den. But instead of going in, he took off. Spooney took off after him, but the snow was deep and it was tough going for him. I was all right on my snowshoes.

The fox took to the lakeshore and then out onto the lake ice. I thought to myself, "That dog is not going to catch the fox on that ice."

By the time I got to the lakeshore I could see Spooney away out on the ice just lying there. He was rolling around, over and over. He used to do this whenever he caught something. But this time I couldn't see that he'd caught anything.

I was mad. It wasn't like Spooney to give up a chase.

"Get after that fox," I hollered at him as I lumbered ahead. "Get that fox, Spooney."

Boy, I was put out. I didn't know why he was doing this to me.

"Get that fox."

He paid no attention to me. He just kept rolling over and over.

As I got closer I could see a dark spot on the ice. Sure enough, there was the fox. That made me happy again.

Spooney was a good dog.

On the way home we went by Joe's cabin again. As we came near he called out, kind of making fun. "How did you make out, Barney?"

I held up the fox.

Joe just shook his head.

During my long life I have had a lot of dogs, because a dog doesn't live to be very old. Usually just ten or twelve years. I had one dog who was very good at retrieving ducks after I'd shot them. Whether they fell on land or in water he'd have them in a hurry.

I love dogs and have one to this very day, just as a pet to keep me company.

Dogs have shared my life. Very often when I went hungry, they'd go hungry too. I remember one time I was away up 75-80 miles northwest of Green Lake at a place called Sled Lake. I was trapping alone at the time, but I came across another young fellow who wanted to join me.

"Where's your grubstake?" I said when I saw how light he was travelling.

"I don't have supplies of my own," he told me. "But I know my father-in-law will stake me out. I've already asked him because I knew you were in the area and I figured you'd let me join you."

"What's your name?"

"Baptiste Douroucher," he said. Then he added, "My stepfather said he'd meet us about fifty miles farther on in about a month."

I had enough grub for both of us until we'd meet his father-in-law, and since I didn't want to disappoint the young fellow I told him to come along.

It was a hard trip with lots of ice travel, which can be hard on the dogs' feet. There were a good number of portages as well, as we headed north toward Montreal Lake. We travelled right across Smoothstone Lake, took a portage to Whitefish Lake and decided that before we went farther we'd lighten our load.

We sorted out our supplies and laid aside a four-pound tin of jam. I don't know what possessed me to buy it. That's something I very seldom eat. I guess I decided to buy it as a special treat when I saw it on the shelves in the Hudson's Bay store.

"What are we going to do with it?" asked Baptiste.

"We'll eat it," I told him.

We had a bit of other food with it, but by the time we finished our lunch we were scratching the bottom of the tin.

After travelling and trapping for some time we began to run low on grub. But since we were supposed to meet Baptiste's father-in-law soon, we didn't worry. We had been staying at a shack about ten miles from the meeting place. On the day of the meeting our food was about gone. We decided to leave the dogs at the shack as we would be returning from Dog River, the pick-up point, the same day.

We arrived at the meeting place at about noon. There was a beautiful sandy beach there that spread along for about a mile.

We sat on the beach and waited.

Well, this father-in-law didn't show up. We waited there two days and two nights. We didn't have a speck of food. We didn't even have a gun with us. We were travelling light so as to be better able to pack the food on our backs.

I spent a lot of time just walking up and down the nice sandy beach, while Baptiste spent his time sleeping.

"If I sleep, I don't feel so hungry," he said.

The water was calm and smooth as glass as I walked along. It is seldom you see the smoothness extend so far out into the water.

All of a sudden I saw something away out on the water. It was making a small, V-shaped ripple as it moved along. I thought it was a big beetle skimming along on top of the water, and turned away.

A moment later I glanced back. It was much closer to shore. It wasn't a beetle. It was the fin of a fish riding through the surface of the water. It kept coming straight toward where I was standing. I'd never seen a fish do a thing like that before. I thought perhaps it was sick.

That fish was swimming full speed to the beach. Even when he hit the sand, he kept wiggling his tail. I was in the water behind him in a flash. I cut my hands on his fins as I grabbed at him, but I had him.

Throwing him up onto the beach I went after him and kicked him still farther away from the water. I didn't care whether he was sick or not. I was going to have something to eat. I was laughing to myself.

Today, as I look back, I think of how God supplied food for Elijah. I am sure He sent that fish to shore when He saw how hungry we were. Never in all my years have I ever heard of a fish doing a thing like that.

The fish was a walleye weighing a good six pounds. Taking it to where Baptiste was sleeping, I hollered, "Get up. I got a fish. We're going to eat." He was sure surprised.

Next day our food supply arrived and we hit the trail again under heavy loads. They were wonderful days. We didn't mind the long walk.

8

We Went Through the Ice

The year was 1924. I was twenty-three years old.

A fellow named Paul Morin and I had been busy with harvest work around the area of Leask and had just travelled back to Big River. Our main concern now was getting ready for the hunting and trapping season which was fast approaching.

The furthest thing from my mind was the topic of girls. But it was at that time that my mother and stepfather were after me to marry a certain girl. A lot of people seemed to want me to get married.

"Barney," my mother would say, "you're getting older now. You should settle down with a girl." She would name this girl over in Green River. She was a nice girl but I guess she just wasn't supposed to be my wife. I think she liked me pretty well, because I received a letter from her one day.

"Dear Barney: Will you please come to Green Lake as soon as you can? My parents are trying to force me to marry a guy I don't want to marry. Can you come over right away and help me, Barney?"

Well, I guess I had a special place in my heart for that girl and it was nice that she wrote to me. So I said to Paul, "Let's go over to Green Lake to see what we can do, and we can do a little hunting on the side."

I guess Paul wasn't fussy about getting mixed up in this girl's problem, but he decided he would go along anyway.

We travelled on the freshly frozen ice of Cowan Lake, pulling a little sleigh loaded with grub, extra moccasins and some traps. Everything went well. It was October and there was little snow. The ice made travelling easy and we covered the first thirty miles in good time.

In order to satisfy Paul with a little hunting, we had made arrangements to stop at a certain place and do some trapping. But as we neared this area I got to thinking. Waiting until he caught up, I said, "Paul, better not stop to do any trapping. This girl said we should hurry. If we travelled on through the night we could be in Green Lake by daylight if we don't get too tired."

Cowan Lake is long and narrow and by travelling in a straight line we often hit a point of land that jutted out into the Lake. One night we made a good campfire, thawed out some of our grub and warmed our hands around hot mugs of steaming tea. We rested and talked awhile.

Refreshed, we set out. After travelling about a mile from where we'd had the campfire, the ice suddenly gave way and we plunged into the frigid water.

The shock snatched the breath from our lungs. In almost total darkness, we threshed about among the blocks of ice.

"Help me!" shouted Paul.

"Paddle your feet," I hollered. "Don't stop. Pump your legs."

Our heavy clothes were like lead weights. We clawed at the edge of the ice for a firm grasp. Paul grabbed hold of me.

"Don't hold me," I choked, spitting out water. "Leave go of me. Let me alone," I kept shouting at him. "I'll try to get out and you grab my feet."

I knew every second we stayed in the water was a matter of life and death. Our jaws chattered so that we could barely talk and the cold water was numbing our hands. Pulling off a mitt, I reached out as far as I could and pressed it onto solid ice. I left it a few seconds. When it had frozen to the ice I slowly pulled myself up. The ice held under my weight. My hands had almost no feeling as I lay spread-eagle.

"Grab my feet," I hollered to Paul. In the darkness I could hear him floundering, but finally I felt his grasp on my leg. I eased myself along the ice. We were out.

The first thing I thought about was my matches. I reached in my pocket and shoved some in my hair. My hair was long at that time. I had learned from old-timers that if you take a wet match and put it in your hair for a while, you can light it. Don't ask me how it works. I don't try to understand it. But for me it works, as it does for many people.

Our sleigh hadn't gone through the ice and we pulled our supplies apart looking for anything that would burn. There was little that would catch fire. We scarcely got our hands warm.

In the darkness we could make out the dim outline of the trees on shore. The distance wasn't far, but our clothes were frozen stiff. We pounded them to allow us to bend our legs and started out at a run, generating a little body heat on the way.

Once in the bush we grabbed twigs, bark,

branches, anything to start a fire. As it caught we added larger wood until at last we were leaning over a blazing fire. We soaked the heat into our trembling bodies. Steam rose up from our clothes as we turned ourselves first one side to the fire and then the other. I think we are alive today because I had learned that secret of how to put a wet match in my hair.

When our clothes were dry we started on the last lap of our journey. We arrived at Green Lake just after daybreak. Our ordeal in the water had sapped our strength and we were cold and hungry when we reached my mother's cabin and pushed open the door.

Her first sentence didn't cheer us up, I must say. "Your girl friend just got married. She went by the door here about fifteen minutes ago." There was disappointment in her voice. "Why didn't you get here sooner?"

We didn't say anything. We were tired.

I thought about the girl as I sat down to a plate of food. I felt bad that she had to marry somebody she didn't like, but that's life sometimes. I didn't know whether the guy was good or bad, but I found out he was my uncle.

There is no doubt that I would have married her if we'd arrived in time, but I guess the Lord had a plan in it all. I guess He knew I would accept Him into my life someday and do a little bit of work for Him before the end of my time.

People soon heard that Paul and I had arrived in Green Lake and wanted us to play at a dance that night. You see, Paul was awful good on the fiddle and I used to do a little calling at square dances.

"I don't feel like going to a dance," I told Paul. "I feel kind of sorry for my girl friend. I don't feel like being happy yet."

"Barney, this is just what you need to get your mind back into a good feeling again," said Paul. "This is the best thing for you. I'm going to tell the people we're coming." He was out the door before I could protest any further.

I was a little bit shy when it came to calling at square dances, but I felt an important feeling come over me when I realized I was more or less boss of the dance floor for a while. Once we got started, I forgot about my girl friend.

We spent the next two days preparing for our return trip to Big River. Two more nights of cold weather had thickened the ice on Cowan Lake and we were in no danger of going through. We stopped at an abandoned logging camp near the place where we'd gone through the ice and decided we'd do some trapping there.

As we entered the camp we found that an old man from Mistatin had taken up residence there. He said we could stay in the building where he was, as it was the only one suitable to heat.

During the first night we discovered we were in for a surprise. At about midnight the old man started shouting.

"It's dinner time. Come for dinner, you lumberjacks!" he hollered at the top of his voice. I guess he thought he was cooking for the lumber camp, but there was nobody there except me, Paul and him.

This happened every night.

Sometimes he'd wake us up and tell us we didn't need to sleep so much. We'd look at the clock and it was only midnight.

We found him working away making a long

building from scrap lumber. There was a hole about three feet deep under it.

"What are you doing?" I asked him one day as I came in from the trapline.

"I'm going to raise muskrats," was his reply.

I didn't know what to say. I'm an Indian but I'd never heard of raising muskrats like that or any other way. There was no doubt about it, this man was not right in his head. I said to Paul, "I think we'd better pack up and get out of here."

"I've been thinking the same thing," said Paul. "I've got to go some place where I can get a little sleep. This hollering is not doing me any good."

We went out and gathered up our traps and headed for Green Lake. My stepfather was glad to see me.

"Come and help me with the freighting, Barney," he said. "I can do with help as the work has picked up quite a bit."

I agreed to that because I liked working with horses. We hauled freight from Big River to Green Lake and sometimes up to Beauval and Isle-a-la-Crosse. My stepfather had been awful mean to me as a child, but now I think I could say he liked me better than his own kids.

There is one thing that I am very proud of. I never, ever said one bad word to my mother or stepfather all the time I was with them. That was until I got married at the age of thirty-one. Whether they were right or wrong, I never talked back to them. They are both dead today, but I am satisfied that I always talked with great respect to them. After I found the Lord as Savior I saw in the Bible that you are always to honor your father and mother, so I'm glad I did right.

I liked freighting because I could take off and go

hunting when I felt like it. One time four of us decided to go hunting in the game preserve south of Green Lake. We weren't supposed to hunt there, but we'd been eating bannock and lard for quite a while and needed a little meat for our diet.

We knew there were muskrats in the lake and so we set traps. It wasn't safe to use a rifle, because the Field Officer was in the area and he'd hear us shooting. We didn't want to end up with a stiff fine or a spell in jail.

We planned that if the Field Officer did stumble onto us we would each run in a different direction. That way he'd only get one of us at the most.

Well, we got a good string of traps set and every day or two we'd check the traps. On this one day I went by horseback with my little dog trailing along. I kept my eye peeled for the Field Officer and had a good excuse ready in case he wanted to know what I was up to.

All of a sudden I came upon a moose who was having a hard time getting up. I thought he was pretty weak and I could chase him with my horse and throw a lasso around his neck. When I found he wanted to stand his ground and fight I decided to leave him alone.

But my little dog had other ideas and started snapping and barking at him. As soon as the moose started to run, the dog would catch up to him and grab his leg. The moose would stop and swing around. This happened time and again.

The moose gradually headed toward the lake. I guess he was going to try and outrun the dog on the ice. However, it was spring and the lake ice was full of holes. I knew if the moose broke through the ice I

93

could get him. I could almost taste moose steak.

Sure enough the moose struck out across the lake with the dog after him. In no time the moose not only had the dog to contend with but the holes in the ice. I grabbed a long pole from the shoreline and sharpened it with the hatchet I carry on my saddle.

Leaving my horse, I ran out to help the dog. I got close enough to the moose several times, but his hide was too tough for me to penetrate the pole. I got him in the eye once and tried for the other eye, but he was terrified and kept backing away. Finally, I backed him into a hole.

Grabbing my knife from my belt I ran toward him. Before I could get the knife to his throat he was out. He caught my dog unawares and sent him flying fifteen or twenty feet through the air. It didn't seem to hurt him. He yelped a bit and came right back to pester the moose. Between the two of us we backed him into another hole. By this time he was tired and I slipped my knife to his throat before he could get footing. I pulled him out with the horse.

We had lots of meat until we finished trapping. In fact, we dried some and took it home.

When I got back to the place where the four of us had our tent pitched, a couple of the fellows laughed when I told them what happened.

"No way, Barney," they joked. "You don't catch a moose with a stick and a knife."

The other fellow was just outside the tent and heard what they said. "Hold on," he told them as he pushed the tent flap aside and came in. "I was up on a hill to the south and I saw the whole thing. It's true, I saw it from beginning to end."

"If you saw it, why didn't you come and help me?" I said. "Didn't you see what a hard time I was having?''

"I'm not crazy enough to do a thing like that. I thought that moose was going to kill you. I never saw anything like that in my whole life. I don't know what's the matter with you, Barney, doing a thing like that.''

He sure ate his share of the meat anyway, I could see that.

The Field Officer never did catch us. So we made out all right. I wasn't a Christian in those days. I obey the laws now that the Lord is running my life. I never want to do anything that my Lord wouldn't like. That's the way I look at it now.

9

My Search For Fame

I've always wanted to be important; even when I was a little kid the thought was deep in my mind. I wanted people to respect me. I wanted them to notice when I was around. I wanted them to crowd in close and listen to things I said.

Many plans went through my mind as to how I could become famous. I even prayed, when I really didn't know how to pray. The priest would say a prayer and I would say the words I remembered from that. The first time I prayed was when I knelt by my stepfather's corral and asked God to make me a priest when I grew up. I saw how people would almost worship the priest whenever he came to the settlement. Word would spread like fire, "The priest is here." People would get their best clothes on in case they should meet him. I thought how nice it would be if people treated me that way.

Though the thought was never far from my mind, the next time I remember praying about becoming important was when I was out hunting. I was circling a lake through muskeg country when suddenly the feeling was on me. I put my supplies on the ground and knelt down by a small tamerac tree. Again I repeated the words of prayers that I had heard the priest say in church. But in my mind was the request I was sending to God.

As time passed it didn't seem as though my prospects of becoming a priest were going to be realized. After all, I didn't have the education, for one thing.

There was one thing I enjoyed doing in my spare time—playing pool. I spent a lot of my time in pool rooms. If I became good enough at this game, I thought, perhaps this would be my pathway to an important life. The thought lingered in my mind that if I could become very good at pool, I would be sent from city to city, playing in professional pool tournaments. I would be known all over.

Things were falling into place. It was almost as though it was destined to be. I found myself in Prince Albert, Saskatchewan one winter with nothing to do. I found a place to sleep and eat next to a pool hall. The name of it was Palick's Pool Room.

The place was usually crowded. I decided to play for fifty cents a pea. You see, there was a bottle with little things like garden peas in it. On each pea was marked a number. You would take a pea from the bottle, see what number you got, and try to hit the ball with the same number on it into the hole. If you did that you got fifty cents.

I played in that pool room all winter and came away with four hundred dollars in my pocket in the spring. There were very few people who could beat me at pool. But there was no way that I would become a professional because I didn't have a manager or anyone to lead me into places where I could become well-known and famous. I didn't have the ability to make my way in the business world beyond the bush country.

Sometimes when I walked into a pool room, everybody would put their cues up in the rack. They knew if they played against me they would lose their money. I did come across a Negro man, though, who I must say was about as good as I was at pool. We spent a lot of time playing together.

The night I left Prince Albert, I went over to Big River. There was a dog derby going on and a great crowd had gathered. Excitement ran high and I thought I would get in on it. I wandered over to the pool room and hit up various ones for a game of pool. I came out of that place with eighty dollars in my pocket. That was good money in those days for a night's work.

Well, I put my pool cue aside and went back to helping my stepfather with his freighting again. This time he was hauling fish. Sometimes we hauled twenty boxes of fish, about four thousand pounds. At that time we used two teams of small horses. I drove one sleigh and my stepfather the other.

Today northern fish are loaded into aircraft which land right at the fish camps. Horses don't do it anymore.

In the meantime I wasn't getting to be very important and it played on my mind as I travelled the lonesome trails. Things were just not working out for me.

Another idea came into my head. I was a good boxer. I'd spent a lot of time practicing since the day in the Residential School when the youngster gave me a licking.

I got two pair of boxing gloves and carried them with me. Whenever I got into a settlement I'd look around for somebody who'd take me on and toss him a pair of gloves. I'd always win. No one ever beat me. So I settled it in my mind that this profession would lead me to fame. I would go far and wide this time. My dream would come true.

I remember boxing three men at one session once. I boxed the first man until he'd had enough, then they put the gloves on the second until I finished him and then I took on the third as quickly as they could change the gloves. My arms were so tired I could hardly hold them up, but I never gave up. They had three men to fight me and I licked them all. After two years of knocking people around like that I gave it up. I just wasn't getting off the ground as far as travelling around and becoming important goes.

My nose was getting the worst of the boxing profession as well. One doctor told me, "Barney, your nose is no good for boxing. Look at it, it's getting all banged up." He had to take a little piece off my nose once.

So, it was back to the bush country for me. Travelling the trails, the lakes and rivers. Once I came across a trail from Carlton to the south end of Green Lake. It was a trail used in the days of Red River ox carts with their two big wheels. Hudson's Bay Company freight travelled this trail in the 1850s.

I had not gone far on this trail before I saw an old man coming toward me. As he drew closer I could see that he was about sixty-five or seventy years of age. As I drew my horse up beside him I realized he was a man I had met years before.

"Frank," I said. "Is that Frank Swier?"

His eyes peered at me from an unshaven face for a few seconds before he recognized me.

"Barney, well, I'll be." He shoved a brown,

wrinkled hand toward me. "What are you doing in this country, Barney?"

"I'm doing the same as usual, Frank," I told him, slipping from my horse and stretching my legs. "I do a little bit of hunting and trapping and so on."

My mind was a little troubled as I saw Frank on foot. He walked with an uncertain gait. He was not a man for this tough north country.

"Where's your horse, Frank?" I said.

"I ain't got a horse now, Barney. I have to foot it every place I go."

I'm not one to poke my head into anyone's business, but here was Frank with no horse or even a dog to pack his supplies. And here he was, not even on the edge of civilization. He was in deep bush country.

"What are you up to these days?" I asked him, trying to see what the score was.

"I've been doing a bit of hunting, Barney." He motioned with his arm the general area to the north.

"Where's your cabin?"

He pointed over his shoulder toward a clearing several hundred yards away.

There was something I couldn't put my finger on right away, but when I got to the shack things began to fall into place.

"Did you get a good catch of furs, Frank?" I asked.

The old man shook his head.

I wasn't surprised, because I didn't think the old fellow was a very good trapper from what I remembered of him.

We sat in silence over a hot mug of tea.

"Barney," he said at last, fingering the worn leg of his overalls. "I'm almost out of grub. I've got to get out of here."

"It's eighty miles to civilization, Frank," I told him. "Is somebody coming in to get you?"

He cupped his whiskered chin in his grimy hands and stared out the dirty windowpane. Finally he shook his head.

"No, but I'll make it, Barney," he said. But there was no strength in his words. "I'm tough, Barney. I'm a bushman like yourself, you know."

"You're not going to walk out are you, Frank?" The old man nodded.

I camped at his shack that night, but I couldn't sleep. Thoughts of the old guy kept staying in the front of my mind. What was I going to do with him? He could never walk out, yet I was heading in the opposite direction.

Next morning I broke some of my grub open and we had a good feed. I always carry flour, salt, sugar and lard with me and sometimes dried meat. It was good to see Frank eat. I happened to have a slab of bacon with me and Frank even wiped the frying pan dry of grease with a hunk of bannock as he shoved food into his thin frame.

"Frank," I said after he settled back to sipping his hot tea, "you take my horse and head south. I'll walk out."

Frank almost dropped his cup. Moisture filled his eyes, pushed out by a faint glimmer of hope. He turned his head away for a few seconds. I knew he was hunting for words.

"I'm a young man, Frank," I said. "Eighty miles is no big thing for me." The words filled part of the silence, but the lump of thanksgiving in the old man's throat was slow to move.

Finally, he reached across the table and touched my arm for a brief second.

I fixed Frank a good sack of grub, helped him tie on the few furs he'd collected and sent him off. I spent the rest of the day fixing his shack up a bit and prepared for my walk out.

I took only a canvas bag of food and a .32 revolver in case I met up with an unfriendly bear. I travelled light. Even a rifle gets heavy after thirty or forty miles.

In my younger days there were few things I couldn't do if I put my mind to it. You can believe me or not, but I'm going to tell you that I made that eighty miles in one day without sleep. I alternately walked and ran all the way. When I was almost there I came to a fence, and when I lay down to crawl under it, I almost fell asleep. That's how tired I was. But I never gave up. I'm like that.

If I remember correctly, I beat the old man home. That's how I helped old Frank. I didn't know him very well, but he was a man who needed help, so I helped him. He was sure glad. I wasn't getting very far along on my road to fame, but I was important to Frank and maybe that counts for something. Anyway, deep down inside I felt good. And when you lead a tough life, good feelings are sometimes hard to come by.

10

Delma, My Wife

From the time I was about seventeen I had people trying to match me up with this girl or that; trying to get me married. The harder they tried the more determined I was to stay free. I wanted to come and go. Maybe I'd want to go to a certain place and hunt or trap and stay in a tent all winter. I couldn't do that if I had little kids to look after.

But now here I was, thirty-one years old and I'd met somebody I liked better than myself. That's what I say when somebody meets a girl he wants for a wife. He's met somebody he likes better than himself.

It happened to me when I was on a trip up in the Smoothstone Lake area. Delma was the name of the girl.

We got along fine and so decided to live together. This went on for a week until the priest found out about the situation. He came over to where we were and pulled me to the side.

"Barney." He put a real serious look on his face that kind of puts a fear into a person. "You should get married to Delma. It's not good, you two living together like this." He looked at me, shaking his head sadly while waiting for the guilty feeling to do its work in my heart. I was like an animal cornered against a cliff.

"All right," I told him. "I'll bring Delma over to the church sometime."

A faint smile touched the corners of the priest's mouth. At least I had gained a little time.

"Better make it pretty soon, Barney. Things don't look good this way."

So a few days later Delma and I got up, put on our ordinary work clothes and walked down the trail to the church.

There were only four people at our wedding: my stepbrother, the priest, Delma and me.

When the marriage words were said, we walked back home. I packed some grub, took my tea pail and rifle and went off hunting. I stayed out all night and came back empty-handed. People didn't seem to go in for what they call honeymoons in those days, especially in the north.

Delma was a good wife. She looked after me and treated me well and I did the same for her.

We moved right away to an area near Sled Lake. This was close to where Delma grew up. I built a nice little log cabin, 20x24 feet. There was just Delma, Spooney and me. Spooney was the dog Delma gave me as a wedding present.

Money was scarce, but I could always make a little hunting and trapping. Road construction was starting in the Meadow Lake area and I was given a job grubbing trees for the road between Green Lake and Meadow Lake. It was hard work, cutting down trees, some so big you couldn't put your arms around them. We had no power equipment. It was all done with an axe. Our pay was fifty cents a day.

We had to board ourselves and keep our families on that.

One day when we were grubbing trees about six miles from Meadow Lake, I stopped, wiped the sweat from my face and looked down at a big tree stump. I think if I could have cut trees with one hand and swatted at the black flies and mosquitoes with the other I might have made it. But when you've got both hands on the axe and your face and neck plastered with insects it's a different story.

I'd had it. I couldn't swing my back to the axe all day long, swat mosquitoes, and support a wife on fifty cents a day. I slammed my axe into the stump and went home.

"There must be a better way than this to make a living," I thought to myself as I tramped along. Even before I reached home another plan was surfacing in my mind.

"Delma," I said. "I've got a great notion to go into the far north. A lot of hunters go into the north and come out rich. There are lots of furs up there."

"Don't go, Barney. We can make out."

We had two little kids at the time. They stood at my knee.

"How are we going to make out?" I said to Delma.

"You're a good hunter, Barney. You can hunt when winter comes."

"Winter is a long way off. We've got to eat before winter. What have we in the house even now?"

"We have flour yet," put in Delma, poking her moccasined toe at a partly filled bag of flour under the table. "We have some lard and salt, too, and I can pick some berries."

I let Delma have her way and we held on until hunting season. I was able to get a moose and we dried the meat. Delma was good at tanning the hide and she made a supply of moccasins, gloves and mitts.

In the meantime I couldn't get this northern trip off my mind. I kept my eyes open and made plans. My first stroke of luck came when I came across an old canoe. Then I found a fellow called Celestine Lafond who knew how to repair these big canoes.

I took him to where the old boat was. "Celestine," I said, "what do you think?"

It wasn't much to look at and Celestine did a lot of poking around while half talking to himself. I think he did some hard thinking for a while.

"We need lots of new canvas, Barney."

"You can fix it?" I asked hopefully.

A look of pride sort of spread over Celestine's bronze face. "I'm good at this kind of thing, Barney. You know that."

Celestine was right. He knew how to fix boats. After covering the canoe with canvas and giving it two coats of paint, it was ready for the water. Celestine smiled as he tested it in the river.

That day I laid plans for the most dangerous trip I was ever to take in my life.

Day by day I laid aside things I would need for the trip. Delma reluctantly helped. She didn't want me to go. One day I came upon her filling a glass jar with matches.

"What are you doing?" I said.

"If it rains or something, you'll have dry matches."

Well, I put it to the side of my mind because I had never in all my life put matches in a glass jar like that.

It was August 12, 1936 when I pushed my loaded canoe away from the riverbank at Green Lake.

Delma was standing there crying softly. It was all I could do to turn around and wave as I cut my paddle into the water at the first bend. She waved back.

I had a heavy load, over eight hundred pounds besides my four dogs, which would do my hauling once I got to the trapline.

It was quiet as we drifted down the Green River and into the Beaver River. The dogs slept most of the time. I was alone with my thoughts in the wilderness.

It was late in the day when I ran into my first white water. It was about a five-mile strip of rapids called Grand Rapids at that time. They were bad. Water sprayed high into the air around us. I took lots of risks with rapids because I didn't want to portage my heavy supplies unless I really had to.

That night I camped at Dore River, below another string of rapids. I was tired. The dogs jumped out as soon as the canoe touched shore. They were glad to stretch their legs.

After setting up my tent I threw a net into the river so we could have fish for breakfast. When I pulled in the net in the morning there was only one fish in it; a five-pound whitefish.

One day as I was loading up my canoe a young fellow stood to the side watching.

"Boy, if only I had a grubstake I'd go along with you," he said. "I'd sure like to spend the winter trapping in the far north."

I took a fresh look at the young fellow. I'd got to know him a bit during my stop-over, but had never paid any attention to him. His name was Napoleon Johnson. He was a Cree Indian of about fifteen years of age. I liked him.

"I think I could get some supplies from the

Hudson's Bay store at Patunak, Barney. You have to go through there.''

"All right," I told him. "If you want to come along with me, I'll look after you." I had in the back of my mind that the young fellow would come in handy when it came to making portages. He looked like he could pack a pretty heavy load.

The trip down the Beaver River to Isle-a-la-Crosse was an easy stretch. There we met two men who were travelling in the same direction. We decided to travel together. Their names were Opekokew and Iron.

Travelling on we came to Patunak, where after a wait of five days we were rewarded with Napoleon's supplies.

Down the Churchill River we went. It was good to have company. Especially when we came to the Dipper Rapids. They flew white water twenty feet into the air. We portaged around them. I'd done a lot of packing in my day, but decided I'd show the fellows what real strength was. I had them lay 250 pounds on my back and started over the rocks. I pictured them standing back admiring my great power. My heart was very proud.

When I got to the end of the portage, I dumped my load on the ground and looked behind me. There, right at my heels was a little fellow, weighing about half as much as me, with 250 pounds on his back. It was Opekokew. I didn't let on I even saw him. He had the same name as me until the priest changed mine to Lacendre in the residential school. The day I saw Opekokew carrying 250 pounds was a sad blow to my pride.

Every time we made a portage I thought about that little fellow carrying 250 pounds. And we made fifty portages on that trip, so I thought about it quite a bit.

On we travelled, down the Churchill River, over to Elbow Lake, Premeau Lake and Dipper Lake. When we came to the Haltain River we had to go upstream. The water was so deep and swift we had to use poles. We'd poke the poles into the bottom of the river and push ourselves along. We poled for eight straight days. We were tired and our hands were blistered and raw.

"Look," hollered one of the fellows, "I've had enough of this for a while. Let's pull in to shore and look for cranberries. There should be some with all these jackpine in the area."

We didn't have any luck finding cranberries, but as we sat on the shore prior to loading while the dogs had a little extra run, we heard in the background a faint rumbling.

"It sounds like rapids," I told the fellows. "Let's stop there and have dinner."

We were a little surprised when after travelling several hours, we still weren't at the rapids.

"Let's pull over and have lunch anyway," said Napoleon. "I'm getting hungry. We can have supper at the rapids."

So we stopped for lunch.

We travelled on until nightfall and still we were not at the rapids. That's how loud they were. It was not until the following night that we reached the foot of the biggest rapids I have ever seen in my life. They were seventy or eighty feet high. You couldn't talk unless you hollered into another person's ear. The ground felt like it was shaking beneath you. It was just like somebody was pouring water from a giant tea kettle. That waterfall was on the Haltain River.

111

We made camp below the falls that night, but it was impossible to sleep. Early the next morning we broke camp and portaged around them. It was a steep climb and heavy packing to get our supplies around those falls.

Not far from there we came to another stretch of rapids and another waterfall. We were surprised to find we could hardly move our paddles as we paddled at the foot of the falls. There were so many fish in the water it felt like we were paddling in sand. The water was thick with fish, like flour in a bannock mix. I guess they couldn't get up the falls and had gathered there.

"Let's throw a net in and get a supply of fish," I yelled, grabbing the net under my seat. I tossed the net in and as soon as it started to sink we pulled it in. There were so many fish in it we could hardly lift it. They were whitefish. We loaded them into sacks, portaged about a half mile and kept going.

Two more days of travel and we were deep in the north. It was solid rock almost everywhere we looked.

"I think this is about as far as we go," said Iron. "This looks like the place where we meet an old trapper." Opekokew said to pull in to shore and he took a sighting of the area. "Yeah, this is the place."

Iron and Opekokew shoved their canoe onto the rocks and prepared to unload and set up camp.

"I think we'll stop off here for a day's rest, too," I said to Napoleon. "Pull up beside them."

It was good to get on shore and stretch our legs a bit before setting up the tent. After nursing a mug of hot tea and chewing on some dried meat, Iron and Opekokew set out in search of their trapper friend.

When the men returned night was just gathering in

the west though it never really got dark that time of the year. Napoleon and I were building the fire for the night and paid little attention until I turned and saw their partner. I dropped my armful of wood and hollered out, "Sam, you old rascal. You know me, I'm Barney. Barney Lacendre. I trapped with you right after the First War."

Boy, was he surprised. He grabbed my hand and stood shaking it for a long time. I couldn't get him to stop talking. I guess he was kind of bushed too, being alone for so long. Sam was too excited to settle in for the night, so we all sat and talked.

It was sure nice. Our campfire was blazing beside the two tents. The dogs were off to the side sleeping. And we sat under the stars talking about old times. Tomorrow would demand every ounce of our strength, but right now, these moments were ours to enjoy.

11

Capsized in White Water

Napoleon and I were on our own now. Just the two of us against the mighty Haltain River. To make matters worse, we had to fight the upstream current. It was a tough job, but my dream of a fortune in furs at the end kept me bending my back to the paddle and encouraging Napoleon on.

After three or four days we came to another waterfall. This one was also some seventy feet high. But instead of a direct fall, the water roared through a zig-zag chute bordered on each side by canyon-like walls. This odd arrangement was called Zig-Zag Falls.

We were indeed in a country of rocks.

It had been on my mind the last several days that we had been very lucky so far. On several occasions we had gone through rapids that should have been portaged, and I felt we should repack our supplies in case we got dumped.

"Napoleon," I said as I went about setting up the tent that night, "I think we'll check our supplies and see just what we have." I put it that way so as not to alarm the youngster.

"I think we should repack some of the loose things, too, Barney," he responded. "I just don't trust this river as we get farther north. I think if we have to run many more rapids we may get the bottom sliced out of this boat."

Well, Napoleon was not so dumb, I guess, and it made things easier as we both knew why we were securing the supplies.

I put fifty pounds of lard in a gunny sack. Most of my shells were already in boxes, but twenty-five loose shells I put in a baking powder can. Traps were tied together and the flour and sugar had to be left in their cotton bags.

The next morning we portaged the rapids and figured we could pole our way along the smoothest section of the chute. However, as we shoved our way toward the middle of the stream, we discovered the water was so deep we could not touch bottom with our poles. The water was also so swift that every time we shoved our poles into the water the current swept them sideways.

"Look, Napoleon," I shouted. "Over there on the face of that rock cliff, there's a long crack. If I can get my pole in that I can push the canoe along."

We worked our way over to the wall with our paddles.

"All right, Napoleon, steady now."

Raising the pole, I shoved it into the crack and heaved.

"Barney," shouted Napoleon, "I think we're in trouble."

"Push!" I hollered.

The current swirling next to the rock face dumped us over. Into the water we went—flour, sugar, guns, dogs, shells, everything.

I held my breath and fought my way to the surface. For a split second I thought I was under the canoe. I couldn't see or breathe. I grabbed at my head where my hat had plastered itself over my face.

Already I was thirty-five yards downstream. Flipping over, I looked back. There wasn't a sign of Napoleon, canoe or supplies.

Suddenly a pole popped up to the surface and swept toward me. I grabbed it and held on. Just as suddenly I was slammed into rocks that jutted out into the river. Gasping, I heaved myself up. Only then did I notice the dogs. They had reached shore safely and paced nervously back and forth.

I couldn't understand it. The only thing that surfaced was the pole. A thought penetrated my mind—I was stranded in this wilderness without as much as a rifle, a pound of supplies or a match.

All at once, downstream, where the river empties into the lake, I saw things popping to the surface. The water was calm there and crystal clear.

Tightening my belt, I dived in and swam for that spot. The supplies that were on the surface I tried to gather around me, but as quickly as I gathered them in, they drifted away.

Suddenly, my canoe surfaced. It was upside down and heading right toward the spot where I was standing on a sandbar. The water was only about two feet deep there and even as I watched I could see some of my heavier supplies tumbling along the bottom and catching on the sandbar.

I didn't have to move a foot. The canoe came right to me and I braced myself in order to stop the heavy weight as it wallowed by. I struggled for a long time before I was able to flip it over. It was half full of water but I flopped in and poled myself to shore.

With good footing I was able to dump the water out and quickly head back to gather supplies.

My fifty-pound box of lard just about tumbled over the sandbar and got away, but I stopped it with the pole. The fifty pounds of butter are probably still at the bottom of the river. I lost ninety pounds of sugar. My greatest surprise came when my flour surfaced. I had four bags of a hundred pounds each. I guess flour is lighter than water. Anyway, the flour was only wet for a depth of about a half inch. The rest was dry.

I'd had about a thousand rounds of .22 shells, five boxes of rifle shells and two sacks of traps. All I was able to recover was half a sack of traps.

While I was busy gathering up supplies, all of a sudden I heard this holler.

"Barney."

I thought I was hearing things. I looked everywhere and thought it must be the noise of the water.

"Hey, Barney."

The face of the rock cliff was in shadow, but as I continued looking I could make out Napoleon. He must have been standing on an underwater shelf, because the water was over his knees.

"Hurry, Barney," he pleaded to me.

"Hold on," I shouted as I poled the canoe over to where he was. It wasn't so hard poling a canoe that wasn't loaded. When I got to where Napoleon was, he just flopped in. Boy, was he happy. I thought I'd never see him again. I was sure he had drowned.

"Are you all right?" I asked him.

He nodded.

"Where were you all the time?" I said.

"I was on the shelf, but I was too scared to talk or holler for quite a while."

He started to grin after a little while, so he turned out to be all right after his scare.

We started in gathering up supplies and laid them out on the rocks. I found six pounds of tea and laid that out to dry first.

"Napoleon," I said, "we've got to keep hunting around until we at least find a rifle. We'll be no good out here in this wilderness without a gun."

We got the idea to hammer a nail into the end of the long pole and use it as a hook to see if we couldn't get some of the supplies that might be in the deeper water.

Napoleon tied a long rope to the canoe and the other end to a rock on shore. That way the canoe wouldn't drift downstream as we searched for supplies.

Now, anchored out in midstream we poked around the bottom of the river.

"Over this way a little," I instructed Napoleon. He used the paddle and moved the canoe according to motions I made with my arm.

I had sighted a white object in deep water. Poking the pole down, I twisted it and lifted. Up came my white Hudson's Bay parka. I'd wrapped it around my rifle. The rifle was still inside.

"We've got a rifle, Napoleon," I shouted in joy.

"We've got no shells," he replied flatly.

Well, I kept hooking around until I came up with a few snares and traps. Then my pole snagged on something else. I worked around it for a long time before it finally caught. Up came my .22 rifle.

"We're going to be okay, Napoleon," I said.

"We've still got no shells."

As we were hanging blankets and a few things up to dry on shore, I noticed something reflecting in the

119

water about where the sandbar was.

I jumped in the canoe and paddled to the spot. It was the top of a tin that was causing the reflection. I jabbed the pole down at it until the nail punctured the can. Slowly I brought it up. I had my twenty-five rifle shells in the baking powder tin. This brought a slight smile to Napoleon's lips. I also hooked up a sack containing a few things, including the sealer of matches my wife had packed. They were as dry as could be.

A day or two later we gathered what supplies we had left and loaded the canoe. We were a little discouraged, but there was new hope in each day.

"We'll be all right, Napoleon," I assured the youngster. "We have lots of flour and lard."

On we paddled for several more days until I figured we must be about in the middle of good fur territory. At least from stories I'd heard old-timers tell.

Just where the Haltain River emptied into a little lake, I motioned Napoleon to steer in to shore. It was a quiet, marshy spot and I pictured ourselves hauling out a full load of muskrat pelts come spring.

The date was October 14, 1936. The trip in had taken us two months.

We surveyed the area briefly. There was a good stand of trees in the surrounding countryside, so no doubt there would be big game as well. I didn't mention money to the youngster, but there was little chance that we wouldn't end up with more money than we'd know what to do with for a while. We'd probably be a little famous come spring.

"We'll build ourselves a little cabin, Napoleon," I said, "right here where I'm standing. We'll have a good winter. You'll be glad you came along with me."

We were in for a big surprise. Trapping was no good. We got our quota of ten beavers each, which we were not allowed to trap at all in the south that year. But that was about all.

Some Chipewyans were passing through the area and they stopped by our cabin. They spoke Cree so I was able to talk to them.

"You're a good hunter," they said to me. "We have never seen a man hunt like you do. If there were any animals here you'd be sure to get them. But this year is no good."

They shook their heads in sympathy with our bad luck.

By the middle of November we were not happy with the way things were going. We decided to hitch the dogs to a small toboggan that had survived all our ordeals and head south for Christmas. We figured we could make it in a month by dog team, going straight across country part of the way. This way we weren't following the river, which backtracked on itself making the distance twice as great.

We got as far as Patunak where Napoleon decided to stay with relatives. I stopped off for a rest as well and discovered a supply plane ready to head out for Meadow Lake.

"Any chance of a lift?" I asked the pilot.

"What, with all those dogs?" he asked.

"No, I'll get a place for the dogs," I told him. "It's just me."

"Okay, but I'll have to charge you twenty dollars even though I'm going out empty. The regular price is seventy dollars."

It was a lot of money for me just then, but I passed twenty dollars to him.

Meadow Lake was not much of a place then. In fact,

I think the plane landed just about where my house is situated right now. It was just a field.

I followed the pilot down to the beer parlor and we had five beers each. In the course of the conversation he told me he was going on to Green Lake. This is where my wife and kids were so I begged a lift with him.

"You'd better pick up some liquor now if you want to take some home," he told me. "I'm leaving in a few minutes."

I got a supply of wine and liquor, but when we landed in Green Lake I hid most of it in a snow bank and just took a small amount up to the Hudson's Bay store where I knew I'd meet some of my friends. They always hung out there.

As soon as I got in the store the manager hollered, "Barney, there's a man wants to see you over there."

I went to the other side of the store where one of my friends was standing off by himself.

"Look, Barney," he said, pulling a paper bag from under the counter, "I've been saving this till you got home."

He had a gallon of wine.

Well, pretty soon I was drunk and I hadn't even seen my wife and two kids yet. When I did get home I passed out on the floor as soon as I stepped into the house.

Delma, my wife, pulled a mattress off the bed and rolled me onto it. In the morning the kids woke me up. They were crawling all over my head yelling, "Daddy, Daddy."

I look back on my life with sadness at all the sinful things I was doing. I didn't know any better. No one had ever told me the Gospel at that time. I thought

I'd better live like the other people so I'd have friends.

After the New Year I got hold of another dog team and started off for the Haltain Lake country again. On the way I camped at a Chipewyan village. The chief knew enough Cree so that we understood each other. We talked mostly about hunting and trapping, but then he told me of an experience his people had when they thought the world was coming to an end.

"It was just after the First World War," he said. "We were camped out here at the edge of Knee Lake on the Churchill River system. It was the only place in this area where there was any grass.

"We'd all made plans to meet on that grassy point of land," continued the chief. "From there we'd make plans for the winter hunt.

"So there we were on this particular day, all camped in tents and teepees. The men had their families with them and it was a real social gathering. Kids were playing about and the men were lying on the grass swapping stories about their hunting days.

"All at once we heard a noise. It was kind of a roar. In those days there were no such things as outboard motors in this part of the country. It was like a noise we had never heard before.

"Everybody jumped up and ran along the lakeshore to see if they could see anything. I told the people it sounded like it was coming from the sky.

"I looked up in the sky; all over the place. Then all at once I saw something moving in the sky, higher than a cloud. It was going straight across the sky. We'd heard of an airplane, but we thought it would flap its wings like a bird, up and down. This thing wasn't doing that.

"I yelled to the others, 'That is what you're

hearing; up there in the sky!'

"Everybody started to run. Some cried. Some knelt down and kissed the ground. One or two hollered, 'This is the end of the world. Jesus is coming to judge us!'

"Pretty soon there wasn't a single tent or teepee left standing. People were all over the ground, crying and praying.

"One old man about eighty-five years old pushed himself into a crack in the rocks. They had an awful time trying to get him out when it was all over."

The chief was looking far off when he told me that story. Now, as I look back it reminds me of what the Bible says. How people will be so afraid of the Judgement of God that they will cry for the rocks and mountains to fall on them. This is why I spend my time going around telling people about salvation. So they will be prepared for the last days.

It took Napoleon and I a month to get back to our trapping area. But it was almost useless. Trapping was poor. We stayed until June and started back. Our dreams of riches had faded like dew on the morning grass.

When we got back as far as Patunak, I dropped Napoleon off and sent a telegram to Delma, saying I was on my way to Green Lake.

My brother-in-law travelled with me to Green Lake. As we pulled up at the dock there were a number of people standing around. Delma was among them. But as we were securing our canoe and looking after the supplies she just stood there. I thought she would have rushed over to me with open arms.

Finally Delma came to us. But she never even looked at me. She said to my brother-in-law, "Have you seen Barney in your travels? He was supposed to be home soon."

My brother-in-law started to laugh.

"Delma," I said, "it's me."

"Barney." She came to me. "What happened to you? You're so thin I didn't know you."

"We had a hard time," I told her.

She grabbed onto me and really laughed.

12

Moose, Money and Liquor

Money ruined me in my early days. I spent most of it on liquor. I was one of the biggest drunks, fastest spenders and roughest fighters around. When I had money, I spent it—all of it. Almost every cent I made went to the beer parlor.

As Farm Manager for the government I felt very important and the money in my pocket made me a pretty popular man. I was my own boss and I could take off and go hunting when the opportunity arose—which it did one day when John Aubichon approached me.

"Barney, let's go hunting for a moose."

There's too much Indian in me to refuse such an offer.

"Let's go," I told him.

It was around rutting season (mating season) for the moose, about the fifteenth of September. We set out with a team of horses, which suited me fine as I was getting fat and lazy from my good job and lots of beer.

After travelling quite a distance we came to Grassy Lake, away back in the bush. We found a vacant shack there and decided to make it our headquarters.

That night we sat listening for a moose call. The bull moose would be calling for their mates at that time of the year, which would make moose hunting quite easy.

The night wore on and John turned in. But I kept my ear cocked. Suddenly my head jerked up.

"John, I hear something," I hollered at his sleeping form. "It's a young moose, off to the west."

I went to bed happy. I'd go after that moose come first light.

But my night was unsettled. There was a flea or beetle exercising on my back. I did my best to get him out of my clothes and settle down, but there was no getting away from him. He kept nipping or crawling around all the time. I kept rolling around in my blanket, but it was no use. He intended to stay with me all night.

Just before dawn I'd had enough. I got up and peeled off my clothes. But I still couldn't find that bug. I guess he must have jumped off in the semi-darkness.

Just as I was pulling my clothes on I heard a moose calling again. It was a bull moose this time. Again it was off to the west where the young calf was the night before.

It was just breaking daylight when I grabbed my rifle and headed out the door. I left John sleeping.

Running along the shoreline of Little Jackpine Lake, which was next to Grassy Lake, I crouched in the tall grass waiting for the next call. There was a long narrows there; the lake on one side and muskeg on the other. The bull moose would have to follow

128

that ridge to get to his mate.

The three-foot grass gave me a good shelter as I waited. My reward came sooner than I'd expected. Hearing a rustling noise, I peeked out. The bull moose was coming straight ahead, calling as he came.

Sinking down close to the ground, I waited, my rifle at the ready. Just as the moose got opposite me, I pulled the trigger.

Down he went.

I'd left the shack in such a hurry I'd forgotten my hunting knife to cut the throat and bleed the animal, so I had to go back. John woke up as I entered.

"I heard a shot," he said sleepily. "What did you get?"

I was feeling happy about getting the moose and in kind of a joking mood, so I said, "Oh, just a couple of ducks."

He was going to roll over and get some more sleep.

"Let's go up there where I shot them and build a little fire and have breakfast in the open," I suggested. "It will be nice for a change."

So we took a little bannock and what-not to eat with the ducks and away we went. I stuck my knife in the holder of my belt as we went through the door.

When we were almost to the spot, instead of looking toward the lake like he should have if I'd really shot a duck, John looked up on the ridge. There, he saw the moose horns sticking out of the grass.

"I see you got a nice bull moose," he said.

I guess I didn't fool John after all.

"He's a big fellow," I replied.

Right away, John started building a fire beside the moose so he could boil his tea and slice off a moose steak.

All this time I was looking at the moose. I could see that his eyes were moving. I wasn't going to cut his throat and bleed him if he was still alive. He was too big. I didn't want a slap from his hoof.

I pumped a shell into my rifle.

"What are you going to do, Barney?"

"I'm going to finish killing the moose," I told him.

John started to laugh.

"I thought I heard people telling me what a great hunter you were. You don't even know when a moose is dead."

All this time he was fiddling around with a few sticks trying to get a fire going right beside the head of the moose. I expected the animal to get up any second.

"All right," I said to my partner. "You know best."

Propping my rifle against a tree, I went off to a stand of dry trees about fifty yards away to get him an armful of wood.

Suddenly I heard a racket. Turning around, I saw the moose was up and poised for full flight.

John took off with the moose just a few feet behind him. They were heading the opposite way to where I was standing. I could see John's hat bobbing along between the horns of the moose, and the steel cleats on the bottom of his shoes were shining in the sun. I couldn't have shot the moose even if I had a gun in my hands. The moose was almost stepping on John's heels.

They headed for the bush about seventy-five yards away. As soon as John came to a big tree, he swung around and the moose went on by. John jumped and hopped toward the shack like a rabbit. Luckily, he made it.

The moose stopped in a clearing about thirty yards away.

Disappearing into the shack, John emerged with his rifle. He had four shells. He fired them all at the moose and never touched a hair.

Picking up my rifle, I swung my sights to the moose's heart and pulled the trigger. The moose dropped.

When I got to where my partner was standing, his face was as white as snow and sweat was dripping off his chin. "Do you know when a moose is dead, now?" I asked him.

I quit my job as Farm Manager and went back into the logging business. I had about forty men under me at this time. There was always money in my fist. Boy, did I ever have a lot of friends. Sometimes I'd go to town with $1,000-1,500 in my pocket and buy liquor for my friends. I sure felt important. People around Big River were sure of free beer if I was around. I guess the money kind of got up in my head and stirred my brains around a little. Anyway, I was on my way to destruction and didn't even know it at the time.

One time I bought ten cases of beer, one case of whiskey and eight gallons of wine. I took it all back to my men at the logging camp. I figured I was doing a wonderful thing. My men sure liked me. I didn't realize until later that when my money was gone, my friends were gone too.

Anyway, that night after I'd brought all this liquor back to camp, I could hear women and children crying in the tents. You see, the men had their families with them living in tents around the camp.

It didn't seem to dawn on me that I was the cause of

all this heartache. All this crying and fighting was because I'd brought liquor to them.

Delma, my wife, would come to me with a begging look in her eyes. "Barney, you have money. Let's go back to Sled Lake. You can buy land and hunt and trap. We can be happy."

It was as if she wasn't even there. I would act like she wasn't even talking.

"Barney, please, let's go home." She kept after me all the time. "Let's buy machinery and horses. You can take up farming. Please, please."

I was having too good a time being boss of the logging camp to give it up. And anyway, the men didn't want me to quit. I felt very important around that place.

One day Delma came to where I was working.

"Barney, I'm leaving you."

"Where are you going?" I said.

"I'll go to Prince Albert with our kids."

We had two kids living in Prince Albert and two in Prince George, British Columbia. I figured she'd go for a visit and then get homesick for me and come back, so I wasn't worried.

Delma never came back to me. She'd had enough of the way I was living, I guess. I'd been married to her for twenty years. Liquor was the cause of it all.

Well, life had to go on. After a time I left that logging camp and moved to another one. Again I had a lot of men under me and made a lot of money, but it all went to liquor.

I got the notion in my head that I wanted to get back to hunting and trapping, so I talked a fellow named Louie Palchier into going north with me.

We travelled along Cowan Lake and into the Cowan River, always meandering our way toward good hunting territory. As we were making a certain portage, we met a man who had a team of horses. We hired him to take us up to Sled Lake. From there we struck out for Beaupre Creek and on to Beaupre Lake. This is where I intended to do my hunting.

My first surprise came as we were unpacking our supplies. It came out of Louie's mouth.

"I don't like it here," he said. "I'm going home." He packed up his share of the supplies and left, just like that. I don't know what got into him.

So I was all by myself until I came across another fellow. His name was Joe. I didn't realize it at the time, but he was a liar and a crook. He's still living today at ninety years of age.

Well, he became my partner. He didn't seem to be able to do anything in an honest way. Even though I wasn't a Christian at the time, I tried to be honest to a certain extent. Now, as a Christian I'm honest in all my ways. I have the Lord to help me.

Joe was spending his time poisoning coyotes. He thought this was easier than hunting them on foot. He'd shoot a moose, rip open its flank and pour in some poison. Now, this was just not done. The right way was to cut meat up into small chunks and spread it around in various places. You just wouldn't waste a whole moose as well as its hide.

So, one day as I was out hunting I came upon some poisoned coyotes. There were a number of them, but only one whose hide was any good. Wolves had started eating some of the carcasses. I thought I'd pull a joke on Joe so I went back to the cabin and said, "Joe, I found some coyotes lying dead around that moose carcass."

You should have seen Joe. He was jumping for joy. You see, wolf hides were worth $35.00-40.00.

133

Joe didn't seem to realize that the moose hide he'd destroyed was worth a lot of money, too.

"Barney, next time I get a bunch of coyotes like this, I'm going to give you half."

Well, to this day I've never seen any of his coyotes and that was a long time ago. Anyway, I guess Joe was surprised when he got out there and found only one good coyote hide.

One of Joe's strangest ideas came when we shot a moose some distance from the cabin. I was going to start packing him to the shack but Joe said, "No, we'll wait until tomorrow and get it. There are no wolves around here now, so the meat will be safe."

It didn't make any difference to me so I went along with the idea.

Next morning we brought the dogs along to haul the meat back. When we came into view of our cabin, Joe shouted, "Barney, look, our cabin is on fire!"

"Let's try and save my guns, I shouted, cracking the whip over the dogs. We tried to run but the load was too heavy for the dogs to make any speed. "Run," I told Joe, "you run ahead."

Joe made a feeble effort for a short distance. "It's no good, Barney," he panted. "I can't make it."

"Here, take the dogs," I shouted and took off. I had a .22 rifle, a shot gun and another rifle I wanted to save. I was about a hundred yards from the cabin when the shells started exploding in the magazines. Everything burned.

I lost about a hundred traps, my grubstake, blankets, everything. All I had left was what was on my back as I stood puffing there in the snow.

"I'm sorry about this, Barney," panted Joe, coming up beside me. "It's a terrible thing that's happened to us."

When we got to where the fire was burning I realized Joe had set it on purpose.

"You usually tie your horse next to the cabin, Joe," I said to him. "And your saddle is usually leaning against the cabin. How come your stuff is away off there today?"

"Just luck, I guess, Barney," he reasoned. "Funny how things work out sometimes, isn't it?"

I knew then why he wanted us to get the moose meat that day. He wanted to set the fire so it would look like an accident.

"Well, Barney, I guess we'll have to go to the Hudson's Bay store manager and tell him about this terrible fire we had," he said. "We'll tell him we lost so many fox furs, so many coyote furs, so many mink furs and list them off like that." He glanced at me to see how I was taking to his plan.

"You only had one mink and one coyote hide in there."

"Yeah, but the manager won't know any difference."

You see, Joe owed the Hudson's Bay store quite a bit of money. This is how things were done in those days. The Hudson's Bay store would supply the trapper with grub and supplies for the trapping season. When the trapper brought in his furs in the spring he would pay his debts.

I guess Joe figured this was a good way to get out of paying his debt. Anyway, he took this long tale about the furs and the fire to the manager. I forget what the manager thought, but he no doubt believed Joe. Joe had a very convincing way about him.

It was too bad about Joe. He had a lot of education, but he didn't use it the right way. We separated, but he is still a friend of mine today. I would never have any business dealings with him again.

13

A Lady in Love

A number of years after my wife Delma left me
because of my heavy drinking, I again found myself
in the logging industry Probably my heart pulled me
back because with my logging experience I was
given the manager's job. This, of course, let me walk
around with a feeling of importance.

Big River was the nearest settlement to the logging
mill. And so every week I would take a boat and a
couple of men and go to town for supplies. Big River
was about forty miles distance.

One particular day as we pulled into the dock at Big
River, a man called Eldon Beade came over to me.

"Barney," he said, drawing me to the side. "I
might have to leave my job here at Big River and
come and work with you."

"Why is that?" I wanted to know.

"It's my wife. She's always down at the dock here
when she hears an outboard motor. She thinks it
might be you. She watches for you all the time. She
has a deep feeling for you, I guess."

It was true what he said. I had noticed a woman
who always seemed to be at the dock when I pulled

in. She would be standing there when I left as well. I didn't pay any attention because she never once spoke to me.

"When you leave, she watches you until you're out of sight," continued Eldon. "If I go and work for you she won't have to keep watching for you all the time."

Well, his talk left my mind until one day my men and I were loading supplies at the dock. This woman was standing there as usual. She never said anything and neither did I. Everything was the same as normal until we were just ready to pull away from the dock. Suddenly, she jumped into the boat.

"I'm going with you," she said.

There was nothing I could say because I didn't own the logging mill. There were lots of families there and I thought perhaps she would live with some of them and that would be the end of it.

So we took her to the logging camp. Her name was Mary Beade. Her husband didn't seem to mind one way or the other. When we got the supplies unloaded at the camp, she looked the place over.

"I like it here. I think I'm going to stay," she said, following along after me.

"Well," I thought to myself, "I'll take her back to her husband next time I go for supplies." I didn't worry about her living with me for such a short time. I just took it for granted that she would go along home.

Sure enough, next time we left for supplies, she jumped into the boat. As we docked at Big River she said, "I'm going up to my house, Barney."

I thought everything was turning out real well. While the supplies were being rounded up, I went over to the beer parlor for a few drinks. As I was enjoying my drink, all of a sudden Mary was beside my chair.

"What are you doing here?" I asked.

She poked a ten-dollar bill at me. "Here."

"I don't want that," I told her, turning back to my drink.

She kept pushing it at me. I thought it was for keeping her for the week she stayed at my place.

But she wouldn't give up so I pressed the bill into my pocket. I found out later her husband had given it to her to give me for keeping her.

I thought the whole situation was cleared up and was glad to get down to the dock to get my supplies loaded and head back to the camp. But just as we were about ready to shove off, here was Mary coming along with all her belongings in a box. She jumped in the boat.

"Well, I'm all ready to go now," she said happily.

She lived with me after that. Even though Eldon, her husband, worked at my logging camp she would have nothing to do with him. She stayed with me.

Mary was a first-class woman when I met her. She didn't drink. She was as clean as a whip and she looked after me in a wonderful way. But I was the ruination of her life. Liquor is what caused it.

She lived with me for fifteen years. We had five children altogether, but Hazel and Freddie are the only ones alive. After all those years I had to kick her out.

You see, one thing led to another, and I guess what brought it all to a head was when I was up north guiding some American big game hunters. We were flown away back into the wilderness and had very good success. I came out with four hundred dollars in my pocket for guiding fees. There was a real feeling of happiness in me as I went to my cabin. Things were looking up. I had bought new furniture for our place before I left on the trip and now this extra money would put us on our feet.

When I opened the door and walked into the house, it was empty. There was nothing there except a little wooden box over against the wall. Mary was sitting on it. She got up when I came in.

"Where is all the furniture?" I asked her.

She didn't say anything. But I knew where it was. She'd sold it for liquor. I'd paid ninety-two dollars for the bed alone, which was a lot in those days. She'd sold it for fifteen dollars' worth of liquor.

I went over and sat on the box. I just sat there thinking that things weren't working out well at all. I wished I could have been a preacher, then I might not have had this liquor problem. I thought too of a fellow named Bill Jackson who had come to visit our logging camp not long before. He was an Indian evangelist and talked of how a person could be free of sinful practices. He said Jesus could save a person from his sins.

Those thoughts about Jesus seemed to stay with me even though I poked them back in the back of my mind. They would come out every so often. I got to thinking that I shouldn't be living common-law with this woman. I didn't know what the Christian regulations were, but my mind told me that it was wrong. I wasn't even a Christian then.

Finally, I made up my mind.

"Mary," I said to her. "Here is some of the money I made from guiding. Take it and go back to where I got you from."

"No, Barney, please."

"You have to go. This is no good the way things are

going. It's not right that we live together anyway."

"Please, Barney. What about Hazel and Freddie?"

"I'll look after them as best I can," I said.

She just stood there for a while. She couldn't believe I'd send her off.

"You go and live the kind of life you want to live, and I'll live the kind of life I want to live." This is what I told her.

She stayed around Green Lake for about a month before she finally left town. Seven times she came back to me and begged me to let her stay, but I was firm. She wanted me to build her a separate cabin on the trapline, but I wouldn't.

Hazel was eight and Freddie five when Mary left. Many is the time I'd bundle them up and take them on my toboggan on the trapline as I checked my traps. Now they are grown-ups.

In February, 1978 I got a phone call from Freddie.

"Mother has died," he said. "Can you come to the funeral?"

They were at Whitefish Lake, Saskatchewan. I thought I should go to Mary's funeral, so Abe Heppner of the Northern Canada Evangelical Mission offered to take me.

Upon arriving, I was asked to speak at the "wake." This is when they have the casket in a house and friends and relatives come to sit and spend the night there. I gave a good Gospel message. I was saved by that time.

A man named Bill Turner was there looking after things. He came up to me after the service and said, "Barney, we want you to stay over and speak in our church tomorrow."

"I don't see how I can do that," I told him. "You see, I came with a certain fellow and if I don't go back tonight I'll have to walk."

"No," he said, "if you stay over and preach, we'll see that you get a ride right to your doorstep."

I decided to do what he said. I preached in his church like he wanted. Seven people came to know the Lord as Savior. They were Indian people. They walked right up to the pulpit and gave their lives and hearts over to the Lord.

After that meeting, Bill came up to me again. "Barney, tomorrow night we're going to have a special meeting in our church and you're the special speaker." Then he added, "On Tuesday morning we'll load you up and take you home—right to your doorstep."

So I stayed again and prepared a message that would open up the people's hearts and minds to the Gospel.

I was glad I'd gone to Mary's funeral.

It was very hard for me to raise Hazel and Freddie when they were small. I guess Marshall Calverly was watching how things were going, because he came to me one day and said, "Barney, I know of a Christian place that will raise your children for you."

The place was in northern Saskatchewan, called the Montreal Lake Children's Home. They looked after kids whose parents couldn't look after them for one reason or another. Hazel and Freddie stayed there a number of years.

When Hazel was eleven, she and Freddie were staying with me for a while. The color was leaving my hands. In fact, my whole body was like a checker board, covered with white patches. This bothered Hazel. "Daddy," she said, "when you're talking to kids in Bible camp or preaching to your own people, your hands show up so much. I don't even dare look that way. I don't like the looks of those patches, Daddy."

"I don't know what to do about it," I told her.

"Why don't you go to the doctor?"

I love my little daughter, so just to please her I did go and see the doctor.

"What is this disease?" I said. "And how can I get rid of it?"

"Barney, it is not a disease," said the doctor. "The pigment of your skin is leaving you. It cannot be stopped. I know of no man that can stop it. Pretty soon you will be all white, like a white man."

I didn't care much for what he said. I was satisfied to be an Indian. Anyway, my heart was already white, washed by the blood of Jesus, as I was a Christian. So I guess it didn't matter much about the color of the rest of me.

"What did the doctor give you for your hands?" asked Hazel as soon as I got into the house.

"The doctor can't do anything about the spots," I told her. "He had no medicine for it."

Hazel went off and sat by herself.

As it was supper time, Freddie and I went to the table to eat.

"Come, Hazel," I called.

"I'm not hungry, Daddy."

As a rule, every night I would take the Bible and read to the children before they went to bed. This night as Freddie brought the Bible to me, Hazel came over and said, "Dadddy, you know there's nothing too hard for the Lord. Let's pray that He will give you the right color in your hands."

I almost laughed at her because I didn't think the Lord could do such things. But I didn't want to hurt the feelings of the poor little kid. So, after reading, I laid the Bible to the side and knelt down. The boy knelt on one side of me and the girl on the other.

As I prayed that night about my hands, I started to get interested. Maybe the Lord would do such a thing as bring color back to my body. So every night we put it in our prayers.

In six months the spots were so small on my body that you had a hard time to find one. In a year my skin was completely normal. I had a few spots of white hair on my head, but that was all.

Ever since that time I trust the Lord in everything. Even little things like going uptown, that I may not run into bad company. That's how I believe in Him. I have great faith in the Lord.

Not long after that I met the doctor. He looked at me in surprise.

"What did you do with your hands, Barney?"

"I trusted another doctor," I said.

"What doctor was that?" he said. "Where does he live?"

"It's a Doctor we read a lot about, but we've never seen Him," I said. "His name is Jesus Christ."

He just kind of grinned and walked away.

14

The Priest and the Pemican

People were poor in the 1930s. There was no such
thing as fancy food even in the best of times. Indians
usually eat plain food in the north; we sure did in
those days. We would take a hunk of meat and a cup
of tea, or a whole fish and a cup of tea. People didn't
eat bread and butter and food from cans like they do
today.

I remember once when three young Chipewyan
Indians were travelling to Patunak where I was
camped. It was a trip of seven or eight days by dog
team from where they started. On the way they ran
out of food. They couldn't even shoot a rabbit.

When they got to Patunak they were almost
starved. They hurried to the Hudson's Bay store for
supplies. All they could get was bread, butter, jam
and such things. It was strange food for them and
they found out they didn't like it.

They heard I was in the settlement and came over.

"Here," said one fellow. He dumped their whole
box of food on my table. "You can have this. Have
you any moose meat?"

"I have some ribs from a moose," I told them.

Their faces brightened up.

"Could we have some?"

I had the meat frozen outside on the roof of my shack. I got a bunch of ribs and put them down at their feet. They just about jumped on the meat. Right away they chopped the ribs up into small chunks.

"Have you got a pot?"

I put a real big kettle on the stove and they filled it up. It had only just started to boil when they poked out hunks and started eating. There wasn't a sound in the cabin until they'd cleaned up the whole thing.

"I'd starve to death trying to eat that white man's food," said one fellow, pointing at the groceries they'd dumped on my table.

Indians have their own way of life.

One time in 1937 I was out trapping. It was during a very cold spell; some sixty below with a wind. Usually there's no wind when it's that cold.

Anyway, it was a very lonely part of the country. If you came across another living soul you would think to yourself, "Who is so crazy as to be in this part of the country?" You could go for months and never see another person. It was rough country; good only for trapping.

So, I was quite surprised as I was travelling around a frozen lake shore, to see a man coming out of the bush at the far end of a bay.

It brought me up short.

The man was leading a dog team. Behind the dog team was another man and behind him was a priest. As they came closer I could see that the priest had his robe on over his parka and he was holding a book out in front of him, reading as he walked.

I stayed out of sight at the edge of the trees. Pretty soon they came upon my tracks in the fresh snow. They looked around but couldn't see me anyplace.

"Hey," hollered the man in the lead. "Is anybody around?"

Stepping out of the bush, I waved and yelled.

As we came together, one of the Chipewyan men held out his hand. He recognized me as he had met me a few times before.

As we started to talk, the priest suddenly hollered, "Barney, it's you." He was so happy to see me. "I'm Father Morrow. We met before, remember?"

Sure enough, I knew the priest, too. He was a white man. I'd met him in my travels here and there.

We had a good talk right there on the trail. The dogs were glad of the rest and lay down in the snow.

"Barney," added the priest at last. "Do you have any bannock?"

"I have bannock in my tent, Father," I told him. "But it's pitched over on the island. I'm going back, so I'll travel with you."

My main cabin was about ten miles away, but I had a tent that I stayed in when I was checking the string of traps in that area.

"We haven't had a good meal in seven days, Barney," continued the priest. "We left Patunak, went away up north to Cree Lake, then north to Churchill and now back here. We've been visiting settlements in my district."

Father Morrow took a piece of pemican from his parka under his robe. It was about four inches wide and six inches long.

"This is what I've been nibbling on for seven days," he said. "When I get real hungry I break a piece off."

He broke a piece off for me to try. It was made from pounding berries, meat and lard together. It gets dry and hard and keeps for a long time.

When we got to the tent I made a bresh batch of bannock. It's made by mixing flour, baking powder, water and salt together. You can cook it in a frying pan over hot coals.

In the meantime, they chopped up some moose ribs and boiled them. Boy, did they ever eat.

"Which way are you heading, Father?" I asked when they'd finished eating.

He told me.

"You have to go by my main cabin," I said. "When you get there, go in and make yourself at home. I have moose meat stacked on the roof and food in the cabin as well. Make yourselves a good meal and take some grub for your travels."

We never locked our cabins in those days. If somebody was travelling and you weren't home, he might stop in and make a meal. If he used firewood, he'd cut more for you before he left. People were good in those days.

Sometime later I came across these two Chipewyan Indians who were travelling with the priest. They told me what happened when they got to my cabin.

"My friend and I went on the roof and got some moose meat, but Father Morrow went inside and ate some boughten food. We stayed at your place that night and set out the next day. Before we left Father Morrow prayed for you, Barney. He prayed for one full hour. He did this to thank you for what you did for us."

I believe that Father Morrow was a great man of faith in God.

I remember once, Father Morrow walked across Isle-a-la-Crosse Lake when it had only frozen over the night before. He had nine men with him and as they were ready to start, he told them, "When I give the word, start walking straight across the lake. Head for the church on the other side."

The men were walking in single file. Father Morrow walked along behind them in his robe, reading and praying. I don't know whether they were afraid or not, but they made the five miles to the other side.

They went into the church and held a service. When they came out two hours later, there were four-foot waves on the lake. The wind had broken up the ice.

Everything Father Morrow did seemed to turn out well.

Once on the Churchill River he was caught on some very fast rapids. It had never been known that a man could survive those rapids. Water was flying as high as fifteen feet into the air.

Father Morrow was drawn into them and had to go through. There he was, standing up in his canoe, working his paddle for all his life was worth. People on the shore couldn't believe it. They ran down below the rapids to pick up his body. But when they got there they saw him riding the white water, still standing up working his paddle. He shot right through them! You have to see the rapids to understand what I'm talking about.

I believe that man was a real Christian.

I will have to say this about Father Morrow, though. He was a terrible singer. There was one of his services that I was at. He was leading the singing. None of the Chipewyan Indians could help him out because they didn't know the words.

But I joined in as hard as I could. I was quite proud of myself. You see, the words were in Latin. I had learned them at the residential school.

I sure helped the priest that day. He was having an awful time.

When the service was over he made a sign that I should stay behind. This was the first time I had ever met Father Morrow.

"Where did you learn to sing?" he asked, grabbing hold of my hand.

"I was at the residential school," I said, "and we learned the songs there."

"Come over to my place," he said. "We can sit and have lunch together."

He kept thanking me for helping him out in the service. I guess he didn't want to embarrass himself in front of his people.

I was glad to help him.

We had a nice visit at his place as he went about preparing lunch for us.

15

I Sought the Spirits

Mary Beade's father was a witch doctor; one of the best in the north. Mary was the mother of Hazel and Freddie. I have seen her father, Frank Beaverskin, put the rattlers of a rattlesnake in his hand, sing, and watch the rattlers as they made a noise. Frank's hand would be perfectly still, but the rattlers would shake.

I became very interested in witchcraft as I watched him work as a witch doctor and as I listened to the stories he would tell me.

Witchcraft had been part of my life since I was a child of five or six. I remember how an old witch doctor used to come to my stepfather's ranch. It's like a picture in my mind's eye, seeing the old man of about seventy-five years jumping down from his wagon and shaking hands with my stepfather and mother. Sometimes he'd camp right in our yard and stay a few days.

One time he showed us a shirt he was wearing when he was fighting the Blackfoot Indians. He was an idol worshipper and worshipped many kinds of spirits. He invited them into his life and gave himself over to the devil. Among the spirits he worshipped was the spirit of stone.

He had given himself so completely over to the spirit of stone that bullets could not penetrate his body. His shirt was full of bullet holes, but the bullets would drop off as they hit his body.

Now, all I can do is tell you these things. Whether or not you believe them is up to you. Many of these things concerning witchcraft I have seen with my own eyes. I am now a Christian and am telling you only what I believe in my heart.

I remember a story Frank Beaverskin told us about when he was fighting the Blackfoot Indians on the prairies.

"It was toward evening when we heard them coming from far away," he said. "Immediately we started digging a trench. There were two men with me at the time and I told them to get into the trench. I stayed outside because the hole wasn't big enough.

"I fought the Blackfoot off for two days and two nights," Frank continued. "On the third day they left. You see, I had the spirit of stone. They couldn't hurt me.

"The Blackfoot leader yelled at me as they rode away. 'You've killed enough of us. We're going to come back with so many men, we'll crowd you out. We're going to make you suffer.' "

The Blackfoot and the Cree never did get along. Whenever they met it would always end up in a fight. The Cree and the Chipewyan didn't get along either. The Blackfoot pushed the Cree into the north and the Cree pushed the Chipewyan still farther north. That's why the Chipewyan are in the far north, the Cree in the middle and the Blackfoot in the south, for the most part.

Frank Beaverskin was very thirsty after fighting and so he took his water bag, which was the bladder from an animal, to a water hole to refill it.

"You must be tired," said one of the men from the trench.

The old man nodded.

"The spirit of stone that you have is so strong," added the man, "that some of it has been passed on to me. I can feel it. I'll help you fight when they come back."

There was no way they could escape as they were travelling on foot through prairie country.

As they were talking, the Blackfoot returned.

The man stood his ground as he attempted to help Beaverskin, but a bullet went through his jaw. He lived, but his jaw was broken and hanging down. He died just recently at ninety years of age, so he must have been young when he was fighting the Indians.

But Frank Beaverskin...they couldn't kill him. It may be hard for you to believe this, but I know the power of the spirits. I was a witch doctor myself.

On the third night, Frank whispered to the men in the trench, "It's dark tonight and we've got to get out of here. Do exactly as I say.

"Take hold of each other's hand and I'll take your hand as well. Close your eyes. Don't open them no matter what happens."

The Blackfoot had their teepees nearby around them. But they went right between the teepees. Frank said the spirit of stone did this for them. When they were a certain distance away he said, "Open your eyes, but don't move from this spot. I'll be back."

In those days the Indians would tie a long cord to

their horses and the other end would be in the teepee. If anybody bothered their horses they would know. Well, Frank went back and stole three horses and the Blackfoot Indians didn't know anything about it.

The three men jumped on the horses and took off. Just as they left, a terrible rainstorm started. Some witch doctors could make it rain and Frank claimed he was one of them. He did this to cover their tracks.

This same man was told by the spirits that if he ever got sick, he should cut a hole in the ice and dip himself in up to his chin. If he did this he would get better. Well, Frank did get sick one time and he did this. But the spirits were finished with him and he died. He could stand the bullets and other things, but this was how he came to an end.

I learned a lot of witchcraft from Frank Beaverskin.

There was one other witch doctor I knew who had the spirit of stone. His name was Tom Blackbird. He and some other men were out hunting one day when they were pursued by some Blackfoot Indians. Tom guided the men into a ravine. There was a boulder lying there, right out in the open.

"Quick," yelled Tom, "put your hands on this stone as you lay beside it. Close your eyes and don't move."

Blackbird lay on top of the stone and slowly rubbed it with his hands. As his hands moved slowly over the surface of the stone he talked to the spirits.

The Blackfoot Indians came rushing down the ravine. Just as they came upon the men, they divided and went around them as they would a pile of stone. Yet the men were right in the open. I knew Tom Blackbird and I know this story is true. Tom was a hunchback. He rode a horse until he was very old.

His grandchildren are still around the Sandy Lake area.

These are some of the men who taught me the art of witchcraft.

Witchcraft is very powerful. With my own eyes, I saw a man take two straws, place them on his hand, blow on them and they turned into needles. He handed the needles to an old lady who was sitting to the side. She sewed with them. This is not like magic that you would see on a stage. It is altogether different.

I know of a preacher in northern Ontario who was preaching the Gospel. The Indians didn't like it, so they put a curse on him. Every time he got up to preach, his voice would disappear. This happened every time he tried to preach. There is a lot of idol worship in the north yet.

There was a lot of witchcraft going on north of Big River at a place called Stoney Lake. They claimed that once a year a form in the shape of a horse would come up out of the lake. Every time this happened someone in the area would lose a horse. The horse would die. I never saw this myself. This is what people have told me. It was not a dream they had. And it happened every year.

I made up my mind to become a witch doctor when I saw what a certain man could do with the spirits. He was the most powerful and evil man I have met. I'll call him by the name of "Mr. Moose," because he has relatives still living and I don't want to embarrass them by using his real name.

Mr. Moose had two sons. Every fall he would tell the people in the area, "This son will be hunting over there and this other son will be hunting in that direction. I will be in another area." The people

155

knew that they had better stay away from where this family was hunting. They knew the power of this man.

Mr. Moose could make up a stuffed timber wolf. He would stuff gunny sacks with straw, mix up a dope and put it on the stuffed animal. The spirits would come into that stuffed animal and make it come alive. It was much larger than an ordinary wolf and scared many trappers in the area.

When I saw how the spirits would work for Mr. Moose, I decided I would be a witch doctor. I would at last be important.

You don't learn witchcraft overnight. It's like going to school, you learn a little every day.

Mr. Moose used the witchcraft in his hunting as well. He made snares of moose or caribou hide; not of wire like most snares. He would dye these strips of hide different colors. A certain color would represent a particular animal. If he wanted a lynx he used the right color.

One day he said to his wife, "We're having rabbit for supper tonight. I'll go and get it." Sure enough, there was a rabbit in his snare because he'd used a certain colored snare.

You see, I am saying there are many ways to have the devil's spirits working for you. It is part of their worship. It's like we would go to church as part of our worship.

Evil spells would sometimes come over Mr. Moose. I remember one time when he and his wife were on the verge of starvation. While out hunting he shot a calf moose in the bush not far from his cabin. Instead of taking it home, he built a little fire right there and made himself a feed. He went out every day and ate some more of the moose. His wife never knew he'd shot it. He left her at home starving. It was in the cold of winter and his wife had no chance of picking berries for food. Why Mr. Moose did such things, I don't know. But I did know Mr. Moose and he was that kind of man.

Only one thing bothered me a little about becoming a witch doctor. I didn't want to hurt anyone. I wanted to worship spirits that would do good things for me, if there were such spirits.

During those days when I was searching for the spirits, many of them came to me in dreams. Some of them even begged me to worship them. I made no promises. I waited until I was satisfied that the spirits were the right ones for me. Even then I waited a while longer because Mr. Moose's life and his evil deeds bothered me. I didn't want to get a spirit that would control me like that.

16

"Daddy, Don't Kill Me"

My father-in-law used to travel with Mr. Moose
quite often. On one particular trip they had to make a
side trip to Carlton as well. It was the closest
Hudson's Bay store from which they could buy
supplies.

They had to travel through timber country pretty
well all the way from Stoney Lake to Carlton, as that
part of the country was not yet settled. The only trail
out of Carlton went to Big River.

As Carlton was on the south side of the river, it was
necessary to use a ferry to get to the settlement.
However, when they arrived, the ferry was on the
other side of the river. They sat on the riverbank to
wait.

While they were resting on the riverbank, they
heard the sound of pails scratching on branches as
people moved around in the nearby bushes.
Glancing up, they saw three of four women coming
out of the trees on their way to the river for water.
They lived a distance back in the trees.

The women filled their pails and started back up the
riverbank. But one of the women held back, as

though she couldn't decide what to do. Finally she went on.

After a while there was this same scratching sound in the bushes. Along came this woman for more water. After she filled her pail she struck up a conversation with Mr. Moose. They talked for quite a while together. Then she said, "Go and get your supplies when the ferry comes. Then come over and camp at my place. I'm a widow."

Mr. Moose and my father-in-law went to the Hudson's Bay store for supplies and my father-in-law went on to other business he had in the area, leaving Moose on his own.

"Getting kind of late, Mr. Moose," said the Bay manager. "You might just as well stop over at our place for the night. We'd be glad of the visit. We haven't seen you for quite a while."

"No," replied Moose, out the side of his mouth. "I've got to get on my way. I intend walking late into the night."

The manager filled Moose's pack with tea, sugar, flour and shells and sent him on his way.

Instead of travelling toward home, Moose backtracked around the trees to where the widow woman's teepee was. He camped with her that night. In the morning she informed Moose that she had a plan in her mind.

"I'm going to go along with you," she said. "I hope your wife won't mind."

"I think it will be all right," replied Moose hopefully.

The following day, with everything in readiness, they started off. Both carried heavy back packs. It was a long, hard trip by foot; up past Leask, through heavy timber country to Stoney Lake.

Moose's cabin was situated on a narrow strip of land between two lakes. When they approached the area Moose dumped the back pack on the ground and announced a rest stop.

"I think it would be better if you wait here while I go home and ease the news to my wife. It would be safer that way."

After greeting his wife and giving her a little casual small talk, he got to the core of the matter.

"I've brought someone along to help you with the work."

"Who?"

"It's a woman." Moose eyed his wife, prepared for a violent reaction. He was surprised to see no sign of agitation. He was very pleased.

"Where is she?"

"Across the narrows," replied Moose.

She put on her coat and went out after the woman. In a short time the two women returned. There appeared to be no hard feelings on the part of Moose's wife about having another woman under her roof. The reason no doubt could be because Moose and his wife had a handicapped daughter, then in her late twenties. They believed that a witchcraft hex had been put on her. She was unable to sit up. If she got part way up, she would fall down in another direction. She had to be carried wherever they went. In winter she was pulled on a toboggan. Portages and hunting trips were made very difficult because of this. An extra woman to help care for the handicapped girl would be of great help.

Time passed and preparations were made for a hunting trip. Supplies of meat were low and Moose wanted to make a good supply of pemican for the winter.

On this hunting trip a number of portages had to be made. The woman from Carlton earned her keep as she helped move the handicapped girl over these portages. One portage was a mile long. Everything had to be carried.

One day as they were making a portage, Moose took the handicapped girl with him. The older women thought nothing about it until they heard the handicapped girl calling, "Daddy, don't kill me. I'm all right. There's nothing the matter with me."

Moose returned alone. It was thought that he buried his daughter alive. In fact, Moose told the story to someone before he died. Whether to ease his conscience or not, I don't know.

The woman from Carlton was very afraid of Moose after that incident. She thought perhaps Moose would do away with her, as she was aware of the murder. She started to make plans to escape. It was impossible to do it right away because they were in wilderness country and she wouldn't survive alone.

As the days passed she became more desperate. She packed food in a small pack and waited. Her chance came a few days later.

"Get the packs ready," ordered Moose. "We're going to strike out this way to hunt." He pointed with his lower lip as was the custom.

The two women rushed to his bidding and broke up camp.

"I'll take the lead," announced Moose. "You two carry the supplies."

The old man lumbered off into the bush with the women preparing to follow.

"You go ahead," said the woman from Carlton. "There's something the matter with my moccasin. I'll catch up."

As soon as Moose's wife disappeared the woman took off. With her package of grub under her arm she was deep in the timber in a few minutes. She was on her way to Carlton.

A big hill just south of Big River was named after Moose. It was a hill that was used in witchcraft worship. No one could climb that hill without a thunderstorm coming up. It happened every time someone tried. Moose was the only one who was able to do it. He showed them how he could walk to the top without the sound of thunder. They respected his witchcraft power and gave the hill his name. But today that hill has a different name on the map.

One time when Moose was on the hill, he fell asleep. This was long before a railway came to the area. When he came down he gathered the people together and told them about a dream he had.

"I had a dream while I was asleep on the hill," he said. "A road made of iron is going to go right by this hill. It's going to end not far from here."

Fifty years later the railway came. It was laid exactly where Moose said it would be and came to an end in Big River, four or five miles from the hill. He saw it all in his dream. It was because of these things that I wanted to become a witch doctor. I wanted to be able to dream about things like that.

When I did become a witch doctor, most of my instructions did come to me in dreams.

Before the First World War, Indians gathered at Waterhen Lake. They made a teepee which they called Satan's Teepee. They invited the spirits to come in and have a smoke. Smoke is used sometimes in witchcraft practices. As they were gathered with the spirits, they predicted the First World War one year before it happened. It happened just as they said it would.

Moose is passed on now. Unless he had a change of life and asked the Lord to cleanse his soul, he never will see heaven. He was a wicked man. He was one hundred percent a devil's angel.

17

The Horse and the Robin

I was now in my fiftieth year. The year of decision.
I would worship the spirits—but which ones? There were good spirits and there were bad spirits.

The robin had always been a bird that attracted me. It was a gentle and beautiful bird. Its song was simple and clear. I decided I would worship the spirit of the robin.

Not long after I had made up my mind concerning this, a robin appeared to me in a dream. It was not an ordinary dream as one usually has. This dream was more real; every word spoken could be remembered.

The spirit of the robin came to me in the form of a young woman. I could see her from the waist up. She had very long hair and wore a band on her head like a queen. She had rings on every finger; even her thumb. She had bracelets, a necklace and earrings. She was shining and glittering from all the jewels she wore.

I remember every word she spoke.

"If you give me something to wear, something like the things you see me wearing now, I will help you with your hunting and trapping. I will also make people give you things. Just promise to give me something nice to wear."

She would come to me time after time in my dreams and always say the same things. Finally, I decided that she was a good spirit. Next time she appeared, I spoke to her.

"I promise to worship you," I told her. "Besides giving you a present to wear, I will promise not to let anyone harm you."

"All right," she said, "you have given me your answer. Now I will show you what I look like." Until this time she had appeared as a woman. Now she turned to leave. As she did so, she became a robin and hopped away.

After that, whenever I went out hunting and heard a robin sing, I would have good luck. If I didn't hear a robin, I'd have no success at hunting. I'd say to my wife sometimes, "I hear a robin singing this morning. I'll come back with meat." It never failed.

There was a robin's nest in one of my buildings one time. A man was visiting and happened to be in that building. He saw the robin and swung his hat at it, catching the robin.

"Look, Barney, I caught a robin."

I rushed over to him.

"Don't harm it," I told him. "Just let it go free, please."

He looked at me kind of funny. I guess he wondered why I was bothering about a bird. But I had to protect the robin in order to keep my promise to the spirits.

The robin came to me in a dream shortly after that and thanked me for saving its life.

Every year I did as I had promised. I would hang

something in a tree for the robin. It would be a headband, ring, necklace or bracelet. I would go to an isolated area where there was no chance of a human walking. One time Mary Beade, the woman I was living common-law with, made a dress for the young lady who came in the spirit of a robin in my dreams. I hung it on the branch of a tree for the robin.

Now, understand this, the dress or necklace or whatever would stay on the tree. They didn't disappear. How the spirits worked through them, I don't know. But the spirits did thank me for each gift when they appeared in dreams. You have to be a witch doctor to understand the workings of the spirits.

An old man from Isle-a-la-Crosse didn't know anything about the spirits. In fact, he'd never heard of witchcraft or idol worship before. He was invited into a Satan's Teepee once when the Indians were consulting the spirits about future happenings. The spirit of the turtle was there. He told them that if they put tobacco in the water as a gift, he would smoke the tobacco and chase the fish into their nets. They would have a good fishing season.

When the old man heard this, he went out and bought a tin of tobacco. He wanted to get in on a good fish harvest. Tying the tin of tobacco in a handkerchief, he attached it to his fish net and lowered it through a hole in the ice.

Next day he pulled up his net and up came his tin of tobacco. He went home and said to his wife, "The turtle never took that tobacco. Maybe he smokes a different brand."

You see, he didn't understand the ways of witchcraft. So he went out and bought a different brand of tobacco and the same thing happened.

If you give something to the spirit of an animal, you put it on the ground. If you give it to the spirit of a bird, you put it in the branch of a tree. If you worship the spirit of thunder, you toss your gift into the air.

Some time after I promised to serve the spirit of the robin, another young lady came to me in a dream. She had long, blond hair that was dragging on the ground. She was slim and small. Every night she came to me in a dream. She always came to me from the west of where I lived.

"If you worship me, you'll never have any trouble getting horses," she said.

It was very important in those days to be able to get hold of a good horse. Horses and dogs were all you had to pull heavy loads. So I became very interested in what she said.

"If you promise to worship me, the only gift I want is a colored ribbon. You can give it to me once a year."

She seemed like a good spirit. She wanted to help me get horses. There was nothing evil in that.

"I promise to worship you," I told her.

After that day, I've never had any trouble getting a horse. I could buy a horse and turn around and sell it for more money.

"Watch me," she said. "I'm going to show you what I look like."

As she started to walk away, she turned into a horse. She was a sorrel mare with white on her legs up to about a foot above her hooves. Her long hair was a tail that was dragging on the ground.

So, I had two spirits to worship—the spirit of the horse and the spirit of the robin. Their promises came true. Many people have given me presents. In fact, many people have given me horses as presents. Some of them I didn't accept because I had no need of them.

After I became a Christian I stopped worshipping the spirits of the horse and the robin. But just the other day as I was sitting outside my house, a robin came and landed on the garden. After a while it hopped over close to me. I talked to it. I said, "Robin, I once worshipped you, but I never will again. Even though you helped me many times in the spirit world." Then I said, "No, thank you, I am worshipping the Lord now. He is my Lord and Master now."

The robin turned and hopped away.

When I was searching for spirits to worship many came to me. One of them was the spirit of the toad frog. He was after me for a long, long time. Even after I became a Christian the toad frog kept after me. I wanted nothing to do with him. He had an evil spirit. There were many terrible things that witch doctors could do with mixtures made from a part of the toad frog. I know of one such mixture. In Cree it means a love medicine.

If a man wanted a certain woman, he would go to a witch doctor for some of the dope. The witch doctor would draw a picture of a woman on a piece of birchbark. Then he would make a little mark where the heart should be. On that mark he would put some of the mixture. The man would then think of this particular woman. It didn't matter where the woman was, she would start coming toward that man. She didn't even need to know the man or where he lived. She just had a feeling inside her that she had to go to a certain place.

The toad frog was an evil spirit and I refused to

worship him. Finally, he left me alone.

There was only one witch doctor I knew personally who made the toad frog mixture. He sold it to other witch doctors. This man's skin was as black as the skin of a toad frog. I don't know if the spirits made him that way or not. It could be. I know of no other reason. That man died about thirty years ago.

There is a mixture you can make up that will turn a stone into powder. Ordinarily the mixture has no strength, but by using the spirits it will crumble the stone.

If you can gather enough power from the spirits you can take on different forms. For instance, if I would have given myself completely to the devil in my worship of the spirit of the horse, I could have put my spirit into the horse and used the horse's body to work for me. I could have gone to an isolated place and lain down on the ground. Then I could have asked the spirit to appear. When the spirit appeared, my spirit would have gone into the spirit of the horse. I still would have been on the ground, like a person asleep. But I could have done what I wanted to do while in the spirit of the horse and then come back into my own body. There would have been a danger in working through the spirits this way, though. If the horse had died while I was using its body, I would have been found dead on the ground where I was lying.

Anyway, I didn't use the spirits that way.

When I became very well acquainted with the spirits of the robin and the horse, they started revealing things to me in dreams. Most were instructions about how to use herbs and roots to bring people back to health. They would tell me of certain roots and what they looked like. Then I would go out in the woods and gather in a supply. Soon I had many bundles of roots for a good number of diseases.

It wasn't long before people started coming to me from around Big River area and from the reserve south of Big River. I would sort out the roots according to the illnesses and give instructions as to how to prepare them. I cured a good many people with roots.

One time when I was living with Mary Beade, we camped in a certain man's yard overnight. He drew me to the side.

"I have a very sick boy in the house," he told me. "Do you think you could help him?"

"I'll look in at the boy," I said.

Going into the room, I found a boy about one year old. They had taken him to the doctor, but nothing seemed to help.

"Mary," I said, "get me my bag of roots."

She went out and brought in my bag of roots. I picked out a certain root to use on the boy. After mixing up a batch, I gave some to the little fellow. Then I went back to my tent.

Next morning the man grabbed my arm.

"My little boy slept right through the night. That sure is wonderful medicine you gave him. Could you give him some more before you leave?"

"I would be glad to help your little boy all I can," I told him, as I went about making up another batch.

After I gave the boy some more mixture, the father called me over to his side.

"I have a four-year-old horse out in my barn," he said. "I want you to take him as payment for helping my boy."

"No," I told him, "I don't need the horse. You

need him more than I do. You keep him."

Another time I went into a home where a little girl was dying. They didn't expect her to live another day.

"Will you take a look at her?" they asked as soon as I got through the door.

I nodded my head.

They showed me to the room where she was lying. You could hear a little noise coming from her. She was trying to cry, but was so weak there was hardly any sound. Her little arms were no bigger than my finger. She was just skin over bones. They said she was two years old.

As I stood looking at her, I could tell what was the matter with her because of the smell.

An old lady was sitting to the side. She was staying at the house.

"I gave her a mixture, but nothing works," she said.

"Have you got a certain root?" I asked her.

She looked in a little bag at her feet.

"Yes, I have it." She dumped the roots on the table.

I picked out the roots I needed and set about making up the mixture.

"That little kid will be better in the morning," I told the people who were standing around watching what I was doing. "I don't mean to tell you that she's going to be one hundred percent better tomorrow, but she will be on the mend. I will guarantee what I say."

Everybody smiled.

The little girl's father was watching me, too. "I haven't got any money," he said. "But I have a horse. Tie him behind your rig when you go. It will be your payment for what you are doing for us today."

I gathered the roots together and showed them to the old lady. "Boil these up," I instructed her. "When the water from the mixture is cool, give it to the little kid. Make her drink all of it. Give her some more tomorrow and the day after."

The next day I called at that house to see how the little girl was doing.

"I want you to see her," said the father as he pulled me inside the house. The little girl was sitting in a bathtub holding on to the sides. She was playing. That same girl is alive today. She's in her late twenties.

That's how witchcraft helped me before I was a Christian. Now that I'm saved I have nothing to do with witchcraft. But I do use certain roots that are good for one disease or another. I learned about these roots from old-timers. This knowledge was passed down from one generation to another. I don't go to the spirits for help anymore.

One time there was an old lady who lived near Debden. When she was on her deathbed, she called her grandchildren around her.

"I know of a root that is good for heart troubles." she told them. "I have been using it to help many people throughout the years. It is kind of a secret root; few people know about it." She motioned the family closer. "I'm going to die soon. I want to pass the name of this root on to someone else, so it will be going down from one generation to the next."

She pressed a piece of the root into the hands of one of her grandchildren and said to write down the name of it. "Keep this root until you find someone you can trust. Be sure you find the right person;

someone who will use the root to help people."

Well, these grandchildren grew up into men, but they always kept their eyes open for someone to pass the root to.

One day they came into my logging camp. I was out with the men working in the bush when they arrived. I paid little attention to them because I thought they were just looking for a job. After talking about different things for a while, I said to them, "It's just about dinner time now. You'd best come back to the cook shack for a cup of tea."

We drove back through the trail to the camp and had dinner. After we finished I was waiting for them to say they were looking for work. But they kept talking about other things. Finally one of them motioned me to the side. He pulled a piece of root from his pocket.

"My old grandmother left this root," he said. "It's a secret heart medicine, known only to a few people. She wanted us to pass it on to someone who could help people with it."

He laid the root in my hand and I looked it over. I had never seen a root like it in all my travels.

"We were talking about it between ourselves," said one of the men. "We decided that you are the man we want to pass it on to."

Nobody spoke for the space of a few minutes.

"That's why we came here today. We want to know if you'll use the root to help people."

"I would need to know more about the plant," I told them. "I need to know what it looks like and where it grows."

"I'll come by tomorrow and bring the whole plant and the instructions on how to use it," put in the man.

I have used this root for fourteen years, just for heart troubles, and have helped a lot of people. Already I have passed on the information to younger men and they will pass it to others before they die. You see, I'm an old man now and I wanted to be sure I kept my promise to pass the secret root down to the next generation.

I have used the root myself, as I have heart trouble sometimes. I remember one winter when I was on the trapline. My heart started to bother me. I was right out of the root.

Taking my horse, I started out. It was a long trip to where the root grew. But I knew if I got to the place, the top of the plant would be sticking out of the snow. The plant grows quite tall. Night came on when I was about halfway there, but there was a shack that no one was using and also a horse shelter. I decided to hole up there for the night.

I was very sick. Not knowing whether I'd be alive come morning, I didn't tie the horse up. I didn't want him to starve to death if I should die.

Rolling up in my blanket I went to sleep. I didn't even take a bite to eat. In the morning I felt better, but I thought perhaps my horse had wandered off in the night. I was very happy when I found him still there. I fed him and had some food myself.

The weather was cold and it was in the middle of winter, but I was desperate for the root. After travelling fifteen miles I saw some of the dried leaves sticking up out of the snow. Grabbing my axe from the saddle I hacked the root out of the frozen ground.

Right there beside a pine tree I lit a fire and prepared the root, boiling it in my tea pail. I drank a good lot of it as soon as it cooled a little. After resting a while I drank some more and carried a supply with me.

I arrived back at the shack by nightfall and spent the night there. Boy, I felt good. I went to bed and woke up singing. I went home as happy as a lark. That root has helped me many times.

I told a doctor in Meadow Lake about the root. He wanted to send it away to get it analyzed. They wrote back and said there was something valuable in the root. They wanted me to get the whole plant, leaves and all. I didn't do it. I promised the men that I would pass it from one person to the next. I want to keep my promise.

Many medicines that you get from the drugstores are made up from roots and herbs. They come in fancy bottles. Indian people like myself use them right from the ground. You have to know all about roots to be able to do this, though. It takes many years.

18

Jet Planes and Bush Trails

One day I might be on a jet plane; the next day walking the bush trails of Canada's northland. I travel in any way I can. It is just a means of getting me to my people.

As a youngster, I used to dream of travelling. There was one dream especially that I think of many times. I dreamt that I was lying on top of a railway coach of a passenger train. I could see grain elevators miles and miles away, just sitting on the prairie. There were no trees; just flat land for as far as I could see.

My dream came true six years ago when I made a trip down south to speak in a number of churches. I saw the prairies, the elevators, the flat land spreading out as far as my eyes could see. Having lived in the bush all my life, it was a wonderful sight.

I became a Cree evangelist after I found the Lord as my Savior some eighteen years ago. I travel among my own people telling them that Jesus came into the world to die for the sins of people. I tell them how God rescued me from a life of sin and witchcraft. I was a drunkard but God changed me into one of His children. Now He gives me the power to do what is right.

On one trip I took with Pastor Cooper from the Alliance church in Meadow Lake, and Abe Heppner of the Northern Canada Evangelical Mission, we went to La Loche in northern Saskatchewan. They were showing a Gospel film at the school there.

I was sitting by myself in the back of the school when a young Chipewyan Indian boy came over to me with a group of fellows. I don't speak Chipewyan, but they knew enough English so that we could talk together.

"What are you doing here?" asked the boy.

"I go to the Indian people and tell them about the Gospel," I told him.

"Well, tell us."

So, I started to preach to them. When they heard me talking, more kids gathered around. Pretty soon it was like a wall of kids. There were 450 in that place. Some were standing, some kneeling and some were crouched someplace else.

I told them how to get saved. "The only way you're going to get to heaven is by coming to know Jesus as your Savior," I told them. "Jesus is the only One who is able to take your sins away and make you His child." They shoved in so close to me that there was hardly any room to move. "You have to be sorry for your sins, repent of them and ask Jesus to come into your heart and save you. He is able to give you strength to overcome your temptations."

This was in the afternoon. At suppertime the kids were still asking me questions and we had a meeting that night at Turnor Lake, some sixty miles away.

I had a hard time answering the questions because one would ask a question, and somebody else would call out, "Barney, what about this?" All you could hear was, "Barney, Barney," from all over. They were sure interested in knowing about the Bible. I only wished I could have spoken Chipewyan that day.

You see, when you speak to an Indian in English, you may think he's getting every word, but he's not. There are so many words of which they don't know the meaning.

I had a hard time trying to get out of that place. They didn't want me to go. I had to shove my way through all those people. Even though I couldn't speak Chipewyan, I guess they understood me by the way I put my words together.

This is why I love to speak to my own Cree people. They understand every word. Just recently I was at a service speaking to Indians. One man came up to me after and said, "Look, here is a brand-new siwash sweater. It's just been knit. I'm giving it to you because I am so pleased at what you told us about the Gospel."

Everybody should have a chance to hear the Gospel in his own language.

We were at a service at Waterhen reserve north of Meadow Lake one day and a white man was with us. He said, "Can I say a few words to the children?" We said, "Go ahead."

He used some high words. Those kids just didn't know what he was talking about. They looked at him, wondering what he meant by those words. It's the same in any language. You have a heart language that you are born with.

I teach in Indian Bible camps every year. I take my little tent along usually and pitch it back in the bush behind the camp. I like to be alone. I don't like to be surrounded by a crowd of people all the time. I'm more at home in a tent.

It seems I'm wanted all over, but I can only be in one place at a time. After the meetings kids come around me asking questions. "Barney, what about the time when Jesus was born?" "What about the time Herod wanted to kill the babies?" You see, their counsellors may have told them in English, but they wanted to hear it in their own language. It makes it clearer for them.

Most of my travelling is in the northern parts of the country. A missionary pilot will fly me from place to place, wherever there are Indian settlements. It gets tiresome for me to sit in a plane every day for a few hours, but that's the only way to get to some of the places. I'm seventy-eight years old now and my only purpose in life is to tell my people about the Lord. I want to do my best for Him.

One time I was flown to a place called Pekwintonea. That's a Cree word meaning "blistered mouth." You see, in the early days when people first came to the area, they got water from a certain place. When they drank this water, they got blisters in their mouths.

I stayed at Pekwintonea for eight days. As well as preaching in the evenings, I spent my days visiting in the homes of the Indian people. My preaching at that place was all done in a little Mennonite church. I preach in any kind of church as long as I can preach the pure Word of God.

On the first night at Pekwintonea a little Indian girl of about 10-12 years was sitting there listening. She was taking in every word.

After I finished preaching, I went to the minister's house where I was staying. As I was sitting there in ran this little girl. "My grandparents want you to come and see them," she said excitedly.

"How come they know I'm here?" I asked her because I didn't see any old people sitting by her in church. "Do I know them?" I said.

"No, but after the service I ran down to their place and told them all of what you were saying. They want to see you."

So I followed her down the path and through the trees. Soon we came upon a little cabin away back in the bush.

"Where are you from?" asked the old couple in Cree. They couldn't speak a word of English. "What are you doing here?"

"I am here preaching the Gospel," I said. "I am telling my Cree people that Jesus came into the world, died on the cross for their sins, and wants everybody to repent and come to Him as Savior. I am spreading this Word of God around to people."

The old couple didn't have any knowledge of the Word of God, so they couldn't pass it on to the younger people. My main job is to preach to the old people who do not know any English. I want them to hear the Gospel at least once in their language. It could quite well be that in twenty years most of these old people will be dead. The younger ones are learning English. So I try to reach as many old people as I can.

One time when I was preaching at a Bible camp, an Indian girl of about thirteen years came to me and said, "Barney, your Cree is too good. There are lots of words we don't understand." You see, they are in-between. Some know Cree better and some know English better. In the end they don't understand either language very good.

Sometimes in my travels I'm asked to speak only in Cree. Other times I preach the message in Cree and then turn around and preach it in English, so everybody gets the message properly. I've seen white men preach to Indians and fifty percent of the words fly right past their ears.

Anyway, this old couple that the little girl took me to see couldn't speak English. My, they treated me good. They even gave me a pair of moccasins because they were so happy I'd brought the true Gospel to them.

The next night the little girl came and got me again. "My grandparents want you to come and tell them some more Gospel," she said.

Four times I went back and preached to that couple. But, you see, I had many more homes to visit besides that one. I told the preacher there to get somebody to interpret for him and give the old couple more Gospel until they might come to the Lord.

The minister told me of a couple in the settlement who never went to church. But when I was there they came every night. One night they said to me, "Come over to our place for supper tomorrow night." When I was there they told me, "We're going to go to church from now on."

There was another church at Pekwintonea, but the minister never came in to have services. A lot of people belonged to it as a tradition, so they could say they belonged to a church. When this minister heard I was having services in the settlement, he decided he'd come in and have services in his church. This was so the people couldn't come and hear the Gospel from me. But it didn't work. Most of the people kept coming to hear me speak in Cree.

On a trip to Cross Lake, north of Winnipeg, I ran

into something a little different for the north. As soon as I arrived at Jeremiah's, the Cree pastor, he got right on the phone to the radio station.

"That Cree preacher from Saskatchewan just got in. I want you to be at the church tonight at 7:30."

When we got to the church that night, sure enough, the man from the radio station was there. We had a big crowd. People kept coming in until the place was packed. They were all Indian, except three white men. Two of them sat at the back and the third one came and sat right in front of the pulpit. I could almost reach out my arm and touch him he was so close.

Well, I was preaching in Cree. I'm not too good in English, but in Cree I can give them both barrels. I was preaching that night as hard and fast as I could get it out. I preached about confession; that the Lord never gave authority to any man to forgive sin. If you wanted to have your sins forgiven, you had to confess your sins to God through the Lord Jesus Christ. I told them Christ died to forgive us of our sins. I said your soul goes to either heaven or hell when you die. There is no in-between place. For instance, you go to a store and buy some stuff. You pay for it over the counter. Then you take it home. You don't stop part way home and pay for it again. It's yours. You paid for it. That's the way salvation is. Jesus paid for your sins on the cross. You don't have to pay for them someplace else.

Well, as I was preaching away there for all I was worth, the white man sitting right in front of me became very interested. He was taking in every word that came from my mouth. I didn't know until after that he was the Roman Catholic priest.

I told them as well that I did not pray to the Virgin

Mary, because the Bible tells us, "There is one God and one mediator between God and man, the Man Christ Jesus." I said, "I pray to God through Jesus, just like I'm talking to you now."

Do you know that as I finished my message and stepped around the pulpit, the priest grabbed my hand right away? "I'm very well satisfied with your message," he said. "It was a good message, nothing but the truth. Tomorrow, I'm asking my whole congregation to come and listen to you."

That man had been a priest there for twenty-five years. He knew all the people. Even though he was white, he could speak Cree as good as I could.

Sure enough, the next night the priest's congregation was over to that Mennonite church to hear me preach. I was there for three or four services and the Catholic people filled the church plum full.

The brother who helped the priest in church all the time came to me one night and said, "The priest told us we don't need to confess our sins to him anymore. He told us to do what you said; to confess our sins to God in the name of Jesus Christ."

In one of my sermons I brought out such words as John 14:6: "I am the way, the truth and the life, no man cometh unto the Father but by Me." How can people squeeze any other teachings in between those words? It can't be done. Jesus is the only way to heaven. Anybody that wants anything from God has to go by way of Jesus.

I don't want to sound like I'm bragging, but God has done some wonderful things for me since I became a Christian. In my travels He's helped me guide a lot of people to the foot of the old rugged cross, where they repented of their sins and found new life in Christ.

I also preach almost every week on the Indian Gospel Broadcast which is heard over five radio stations in the Cree Indian language. I've been doing this for about eight years now. This program is put on by the Northern Canada Evangelical Mission. They have missionaries all across the north in Indian settlements. Many articles and a few books have been written about me, and I have played the lead role in a Christian film called **Silent Thunder**. I give all praise to God. There is nothing special about me. I am just an Indian that God saved from sin.

I've paddled the swift rivers that lace together the jewelled lakes. I've bent my back to heavy packs on hundreds of portages and snowshoed through the frigid, isolated wilderness in search of fur-bearing animals and big game. And for fifty years I did it with an empty heart. I thought it was fame that I needed. But when my search was over, I found it was Christ. He filled my heart with peace and hope and lifted the heavy load of sin from my shoulders.

While once I was a full-time trapper, I now use the Bible and trap men for Christ. While once I guided men into big game country, I now guide them to the foot of the cross.

The years hang heavy on me now. Soon I shall never walk the bush trails again. Rather, with firm, brisk step I shall walk on streets of gold in the splendor of the glory of the presence of my Lord.

I shall not need my tea pail or my blanket or my rifle.

Distribute 50 Copies of this
Unusual Book at a
Very Special Price

The Bushman and the Spirits is one of the best selling books ever published by Horizon House.

Thousands of copies have been sold and additional thousands have been given away.

To make it easy for you to be involved, we have packed this book in cases of 50 copies and we are offering what we call a "Caring Christians Discount" of 50 percent. *Your case will cost only $98.75* plus shipping and handling. Here is

THE CARING CHRISTIAN DISCOUNT OF 50%

on one case of
The Bushman and the Spirits
(For larger discounts on quantity orders, call (619) 325-1770)

Please clip and mail

Please send your check along with your name and address to the Caring Christians Plan, Horizon House, Box 600, Beaverlodge, AB Canada T0H 0C0.

Name_____

Address _____

City _____ Zip _____

Please send me _____case(s) of *The Bushman and the Spirits*.

I enclosed herewith $105.00 for each case ordered. I understand that these books are not to be sold, but given away.

(50 books at $3.95 each, less 50%, . . . $98.75. Please add $6.25 for postage and handling on each case, total, $105.00.)
